AWAKEN YOUR
INNER WISDOM

—•—◆—•—

BK JAYANTI

BRAHMA KUMARIS
WORLD SPIRITUAL UNIVERSITY   BKIS

ISBN: 978-1-84694-497-0

First published in 2010 by Brahma Kumaris Information
Services Ltd, Global Co-operation House, 65 Pound Lane,
London NW10 2HH

Designed by Sameer Patro

AWAKEN YOUR
INNER WISDOM

—•◆•—

BK JAYANTI

CONTENTS

FOREWORD

OUR THIRST FOR KNOWLEDGE

For thousands of years, in their thirst for knowledge, human beings have wanted to explore the outer dimensions of the world and reach the very extremes of our universe. But equally, we have been interested to explore "inner space" and journey within ourselves, to discover the secret knowledge that lies deep within. Philosophers and mystics in every culture and civilization have tried to discover the meaning of life outside ourselves, but also the significance of life within. The teachings of Raja Yoga comprise an ancient system of understanding the self. The knowledge was written down several thousands of years ago, but the true significance of the teachings has still not been understood. At the present time, a modern interpretation of Raja Yoga is being offered by the Brahma Kumaris Spiritual University, based on the knowledge taught through the instrument of the founder father, Brahma Baba. These teachings are eternal and yet absolutely relevant to this moment in time. How is this knowledge taught? Firstly, spiritual knowledge is imparted, and this is backed up with the encouragement to practise meditation – because it is through the practice of inner silence that one can validate for oneself the concepts and abstract notions encountered in the spiritual knowledge. Thirdly, together with the study of knowledge and the practice of meditation, it is important to apply these truths to one's lifestyle, practising those ideas through one's daily routine and responsibilities. Fourthly, one becomes aware of offering a service to humanity so that we live life not simply for ourselves, but use our knowledge, talents, skills, energy and resources to serve others. These four subjects, then – study, meditation, inculcation and service – comprise the basic subjects of the Spiritual University. The most fundamental of all of these aspects is, of course, the awareness of the wise self that lies within each of us. This book will help you to find the seed of your wise self, to sow it and to nurture it until it grows into a tree of strength that will provide fruit not only for you, but it will help to inspire and help all those you come into contact with everyday.

BK Jayanti

THE TREE OF WISDOM

Trying to understand the deep secrets of the universe has been an exercise that has engaged humanity through the centuries. We have spent many hours, days and nights thinking, pondering, discussing and trying to unravel all the different mysteries. In this quest for knowledge a few symbols recur, pervading all the different cultures. One of these is the symbol of the tree. In terms of the natural world around us, the image of the seed and the tree is very powerful because it seems to share with us the secrets of eternity. Where did the first seed come from? The seed must have come from the tree, but where did the tree come from? It must have come from the seed. You begin to see how this concept of seed and tree, and another seed, and another tree, actually leads us into thinking of the world as a cycle that moves us into the dimension of eternity.

THE SEED OF PERFECT KNOWLEDGE

In terms of this human world of ours, who is the seed? I think all religions that are theistic would agree that the seed of this human world tree is God the Supreme, the Being who is absolute. The

Being who is beyond birth and death, the Being who is the Ocean: the Ocean of Love, the Ocean of Knowledge and the Ocean of Peace. The One with total wisdom, the One with absolute purity, the Mother, the Father, the Friend, the Beloved, the Teacher, the Guide, the Liberator, the Supreme.

Within this image of the tree, perhaps the most important aspect is ensuring that every single part of the tree stays connected with the seed, and so stays connected to the roots. Out of the seed emerge first the roots and then a tiny little seedling. Out of that very small start grows a tree with a strong foundation, a stable trunk, powerful branches and a myriad of leaves. When one stands back and looks at this huge tree one can appreciate beauty, strength, fullness – and most of all perfect symmetry and perfect harmony. This is perfect wisdom.

KNOWLEDGE THROUGH HISTORY

In terms of the tree of humanity, the trunk is that period in history when there was perfect harmony and unity, a world of total oneness. This was a time when religion was a righteous way of living and when government was natural and easy because each divine being governed him - or herself. It was a time when each human was a sovereign of the senses, a sovereign of the self. And so the sovereignty in the world created a universe of total love, harmony and peace, justice and truth.

However, as the tree grew from that one solid foundation and trunk, branches emerged. There was a need for branches because there came a moment when there was no longer such inner strength and power, and souls no longer followed that righteous code of conduct in a natural way in their lives. So there was a need for religion externally: there was a need for guidance to be given through preachers, pundits, priests and teachers, as well as through the word of law. It was at that moment that duality entered the world. From the oneness of *satyug* and *tretayug* – the golden and silver ages – we moved into *dwaparyug* - the duality of division, where disunity and disharmony began. At that time we began our search for God. In the days when religion was the natural way of living there was no need for external religion. Our own divine spirit – our own inner being – moved us in the direction of truth. Only at the point where we lost touch with that original inner truth were we taken in by many illusions. It was at that point that we needed God, that we started to look for God and that we prayed to God. We didn't understand God, but we needed God because this was the time that suffering began.

WISE MESSENGERS

In the period of the trunk, where there was oneness, life was simply joyful. There was no pain and no kind of suffering, whether mental or physical. Now in a world of duality and division, disunity and disharmony, our own conscience was split. We were no longer guided by our inner instinct of truth and wisdom; the mind was divided against itself. At one moment we would understand, and the next moment forget, and this duality within created discord without. We looked for God, but didn't know where to find God, and so God sent messengers. Among the very first of those messengers was Abraham, and the message that came from God was the message of law. We had to understand the divine laws we needed to observe if we were to return to a state of happiness again. So that branch, later described as the branch of Judaism, began. It was a branch filled with strength and filled with the power of the law; it was the branch that offered support. It taught us laws relating to our relationship with God; laws relating to all relationships with others around us. It offered guidance as darkness began to fall.

From another direction came another messenger, the prophet Buddha, and the path he showed was the path of non-violence because humanity had entered an era of violence. From that original period where the divine way of life was totally non-violent, now violence had become very much a part of life. So the path of the Buddha showed us the path of non-violence and righteous living.

Human beings get so caught up in the law that they sometimes forget the spirit of the law. We get confused when given just the words and the text of the law. In a certain part of the world this happened, and in those conditions and situations another messenger arrived – a messenger given the name Jesus Christ. The message that he brought was a very simple one: that God the parent is the God of love. Laws are important for our life, but yet more important than the law, or rather the ability to be able to follow the law, is the experience of God's love. So the message of Christ was the reminder that my Parent, the Seed of the tree, God the Supreme, is the God of Love.

In another part of the world, where there had already been much confusion, further messengers came, including the teacher Shankaracharya, sharing the message of renunciation. Life had become materialistic; life had become one in which one was subservient to the senses – there was no concern for things of the spirit. The message of Shankaracharya was a message of renunciation; a reminder to come back to the path of purity.

Meanwhile, human minds became so focused on the image of Christ that the messenger was being remembered, but the message had been forgotten. Human minds that are already influenced by body consciousness – by the dictates of matter – then focus their attention on other human beings. It becomes difficult to remember the abstract and to turn to the Supreme, the Divine and the Incorporeal.

So again came another messenger with a very simple message: the message of Islam, which is one of surrender. A message that reminds us to focus on the One Supreme; that there can be none greater than God; that it is Allah the Incorporeal, the Supreme that we must remember. And that we must rise beyond human faces and images and focus simply on the Supreme.

LOSS OF KNOWLEDGE

So through that period as the tree grew, the branches spread out and offered succour and strength to all the different leaves of the tree. When the branches first started they had that strength, but the tree continued to grow and beyond that period described as the copper age we reached the iron age: a time of great decay. A time when the branches were no longer strong and unified, but had sub-divided into many smaller branches, which had sub-divided further into tiny little twigs. By this time the leaves at the end of those sub-branches and twigs where no longer receiving sustenance from the seed, or root of the tree. The connection with the divine Seed was very far away and attention had become focused on philosophy, theology, ritual and superstition. So much blind faith had by now begun. There was great darkness all around and the leaves were suffering; they no longer had that freshness, that sparkle, that brightness; they were reaching a point of decay. The branches were no longer able to give that support.

Does this story remind you of something you see happening around you today? Instead of a world of righteousness and religion, we seem to live in a world of unrighteousness and irreligiousness. And so whichever branch of the tree I belong to, I no longer follow the directions of that branch. I no longer understand the deep secrets of the reality of the truth, and because of this I find myself disconnected from God – disconnected from the Seed – and I lack the experience of love, joy and power. This is the time that the world of humanity is experiencing at the present moment: a time of darkness and tremendous suffering. No longer do the leaves receive any sustenance. Instead, a strange phenomenon is happening: we try to pull the leaves off one of the branches and stick them onto another of the branches. You may laugh and say, "Well that's impossible," and it's true that it is impossible, and yet this is precisely what human beings are trying to do. When we try to convert from one branch of religion to another, we remove a leaf that belongs to a specific branch and try to stick it onto another branch. Of course the leaf is not able to gain real nourishment, so it withers and dies. The reality is that every branch is important, every branch has purpose and value and significance. So whichever religion it is that I belong to, it's important that I should understand the value of my own religion. But equally, I should acknowledge and recognize the value of every one of the other religions.

FINDING OUR WAY BACK

Perhaps the most important aspect of the tree for us, is not only to recognize the branches and their strength, but to have a relationship with the Seed. When the tree has reached its point of decay – when it is falling down – before it actually falls, it puts out new seed, so that there can be perpetuity and continuity. So out of the old tree, we can make contact with the Seed again and a new sapling begins to grow. This is the period we are now passing through.

We can see how much has changed from twenty years ago, when God was not a subject for discussion. Today, people are once again interested to know about God. God has become a focus of our conversations. We are again searching for the Seed; we want to have a relationship with the Seed so that we can draw from it the sustenance we require, whatever religion we belong to. Perhaps it would be useful to think a little about what the word "religion" actually means. It is thought by many to derive from the Latin word *religio*, meaning "to connect", "to join" or "to link together". So whatever religion I belong to, the purpose of that religion is actually to bring me back into a relationship with God – so that I am able to return to my original state once again. At this point, we ask the question, "What purpose is religion actually serving?" It seems as if religions have become a cause of great discontent and friction, to the point where many of the world's wars seem to be based on religion, and yet the reminder of religion is that I have to connect with the Seed.

Through my own personal relationship and communication – my connection with the Seed – I am able to draw back within myself the qualities that the Seed possesses. The Seed has the power to sustain the entire tree, so this is what I need at this moment. A leaf can't be sustained by another leaf. One might laugh and say, "Of course this is illogical; it's impossible to expect that," and yet this is what we happen to be doing. We keep thinking that human beings can give us support and sustenance. We forget that the leaves can only be sustained when there is a clear, straight and natural connection with the Seed, with the roots. What I have to do is to make that link so that I am able to fill myself with God's purity, power and perfect wisdom once again.

A TIME TO GAIN UNDERSTANDING

At a time when everything seems to be falling down and breaking down, there are opportunities for replanting, renewal and transformation. As we make that connection with the Seed – coming back to the state in which we experience a connection with God – so we are able to be part of the roots. Not only does this bring about a transformation for ourselves, but as we make that link with the

Seed, we are able to be part of the roots for the next generation; for the new world that lies ahead, a world of unity. Roots are invisible, they are incognito, and yet the roots are the very foundation of the entire tree. So the work we do at this point is work of inner transformation – not visible, extravagant or external, just quietly, making a connection with God and transforming our selves. So that not only do we take strength from God for ourselves, but we are also able to give that strength and support to the whole world.

This is the time for laying the foundation of the new tree within our own consciousness. Gaining in knowledge about your own role and understanding your relationship with God will enable you to do the things that you need to do, so that a wiser civilization, and a new and better world, can be created.

Let us start our journey through this book to inner wisdom by making that connection with the Seed and meditate on the roots, or foundation, of the tree of life.

MEDITATION

Sitting quietly, letting my body become still, I move the thoughts of my mind in a very specific direction. I move my thoughts to the awareness of my own original form of the seed... and I make contact with the Supreme, the Seed of the entire world tree.

Within this being – the Supreme, the Seed – lies everything: all knowledge, all power, total love. While in connection with the Seed, I fill myself with all this from the Supreme.

And God's power, and God's love, reach out into the universe. I, as the instrument, receive God's light and love... and then it is distributed and shared. Keeping my connection with the Seed, I come back to the awareness of my responsibilities and my role, but now I keep this connection with God alive and real, so that it influences me in all the other things I need to do.

PART 1

SOWING
THE SEED OF
WISDOM

"The first step of Raja Yoga meditation is turning the mind inward; directing our thoughts to be able to acknowledge and, further, be able to actually discipline and channel this enormous potential of energy that each one of us possesses."

What is education? One lovely definition is being able "to draw out" that which is within us – the English word "education" derives from the Latin *ducacre*, meaning "to lead, draw or bring" and *e*, meaning "out". If we wish to be educated, then, we must trustingly assume that we have, at our core, both sound qualities and a bank of well-judged experiences and knowledge. But what gives us the faith that there is this fund of wisdom within us?

Perhaps we believe because, when we look within, the fruits of this wisdom are manifest; there we find a recognition and understanding of beauty and truth together with harmony, joy, love, peace, purity and goodness.

We see very little of the fruits of wisdom when we look outside, however; there, confusion and conflict seem to dominate. However, we do know and sense these various fruits in our inner state of being. And this gives us hope for the future. That which lies within – particularly when it lies at the very deep level of the unconscious mind – is usually very real. It is not physical, yet still it has substance. So how do we access that goodness? How do we bring it to fruition and also bring it out into the open?

The first step is to look at the quality of the seeds we are planting. Every thought and action is a seed that we plant in the moment and, from each of those seeds a whole tree will grow. Whether that tree yields sweet fruit or bitter fruit depends on the quality of the seed. By following the thoughts and meditations in the next few chapters of the book, you will learn how to make sure that the quality of your seed is first-class.

The next step is to find out what these seeds need in order to flourish within the human soul. What must we learn in order to produce the well-prepared ground that will allow this little seed to grow? Such information is, of course, very useful *but*, like most information, it is mainly to do with the physical world. How do we delve deeper than this? How do we find out more about the non-physical aspects of life and wisdom, such as questions of right and wrong or of the self and consciousness? From whence does this wisdom come? Can it really be within us?

MY OWN STORY

There came a time in my life when questions unrelated to the physical dimension became very important to me. It was then that I realized that I wanted to explore knowledge of the spiritual dimension. So I began my journey with questions that related to the self, to consciousness and to conscience and then, further on my path, even to the concept of God. My journey hadn't begun with question about the divine, but, as I travelled, I came to my own understanding of God's existence and realized how very significant and important for me this was.

I speak of my personal experience because the subtle dimension of spirituality is beyond the understanding of the senses. We can see and touch the physical things of the world but we have no such proof of spiritual things. Our only evidence comes by sharing the experiences that have made that subtle, spiritual dimension absolutely real for us.

As I began to study aspects of spiritual knowledge, my study not only satisfied my curiosity, it was actually opening avenues that I could explore and in which I would have my own direct experience. There came a point when information about the nature of the soul – and about the mind and personality as aspects of the soul – was not just more information, but an awareness of a profound truth that related to my spiritual knowledge of myself.

As I began to experiment with that awareness and validate it for myself, I could see that something very deep was stirring within me. I think, today, I would identify it as the stirrings of wisdom, but then I didn't recognize it as such. But when I look back, I know the choices I made at that time were right because a wisdom was beginning to surface that allowed the true nature of my soul to emerge. And so the preparation of the ground in which the seed of wisdom would be sown – in the first of many fields – came about simply through the desire to know; the urge to seek knowledge. For me, the link between knowledge and wisdom is a personal experience: knowledge becomes transmuted into wisdom through personal experience. Knowledge is always out there, but only when I experiment with it and let it become meaningful to my entire being does it invoke my inner wisdom to emerge.

SOWING YOUR OWN SEEDS

A huge amount of information or knowledge is available out there – indeed, we have libraries everywhere. That information could very easily stay in those books without influencing people's lives. The information is out there, then, but you will only begin to absorb the knowledge contained within it when you begin to want knowledge. The desire to seek that knowledge has to come from within.

Generally, we are unaware of the tremendous energy that we have within our own beings. We allow our mind to be distracted by all the things that are outside us. We don't generally acknowledge that the soul itself is the creator of its own thoughts, its own feelings and even its own personality. Our life is usually based on a series of reactions to everything that is happening to us from the external world of stimuli. Raja Yoga meditation teaches you how to become the creator of your own thoughts and feelings, and even to create the type of personality you would like to have. Through a very simple practice of turning your mind inward and being able to direct your thoughts, you become able to become your own creator and discover the knowledge within you.

Firstly, in meditation, you become aware that your soul is a separate entity from the physical body – you become aware of it as a point of light. This enables you to change the image you have of yourself, and have the awareness of your eternal image. The more you do this, the more you will find that your whole life is filled with light and peace. These characteristics of the soul then start to express themselves in your thoughts, words and actions, your behaviour and your life. This is a very easy transformation; it requires no struggle, no conflict, no battle, simply a natural, smooth transition.

Let us explore further what this point of light actually contains within itself. It is clear that the physical visible body is simply an instrument, but the one who is actually operating the instrument is invisible: is non-physical, metaphysical or spiritual. In meditation you become aware that the characteristics of this inner being are beyond time and space. It is something subtle, beyond physical definitions. By looking at what is happening within your own mind, you discover that this is an energy that is timeless, too. Within the space of one second you can have a thousand different thoughts, or in the space of sixty seconds you can hold one thought. Time and thoughts are not equivalent to each other. Equally, your thoughts transcend time in terms of past and future. Within a moment you can look at yesterday or at your childhood or at what happened five years ago. In the next moment you can look at tomorrow and make a prediction of what it holds. Or you can go further, predicting what may be happening next year, or look beyond all definitions of time and into eternity. You come to appreciate the mind's enormous capacity to cover distance and speed. One moment you can be in New York and the next moment in Delhi. We put a high value on speed. If something is fast it is generally very expensive. We equate value with time and speed – and in those terms the mind is the most valuable of all instruments. It's faster than the speed of sound and even faster than the speed of light. Even before the eyes can make contact and create any images, the mind can perceive a presence, picking up in a subtle way the vibrations radiated by another person before they walk through the door.

Your inner being has all these amazing qualities. So what is it? In itself it is infinite – beyond limit and beyond measurement. The only form that fits all the different criteria is the form of a point. It exists, it is eternal, it cannot be subdivided any further. So who am I and who are you? We are this point of light, and within the point of light we have this aspect which is described as "the mind". To start exploring this hidden aspect of your inner wisdom, try the following practical exercise in meditation. Sit quietly with your eyes open and have someone slowly read the words to you, or record them and play them back as you sit in silence.

MEDITATION

I allow the body to sit quietly... I become aware of the many different energies that make up life. As my body sits quietly, I am aware of the physical – the biological – energies of this valuable instrument of mine.

For a little while, I turn my attention away from my physical energies and focus my energy inward. Consciously, I allow this physical instrument of mine to let go of the tension in the muscles of my feet, my legs, my back, my arms, my shoulders, my neck and even the muscles in my face. I let go of the tension of hanging on, and everything becomes calm and relaxed... and now, instead of looking outward, I allow my mind to look within. I can see the world outside, but I choose, for a few moments, not to see it. I let the sounds of the external world fade into the background so that they are no longer a distraction... and on the screen of my mind, I visualize a point of light. I can locate this point of light specifically. As my body sits quietly, I become aware of my life force – the source of life in the centre of my forehead, just behind my forehead. This is who I am... I am a point of eternal light. In this awareness of my eternal form, I gather the full force of my energy within. I know I am the master of this physical instrument. I can now direct the way in which my physical senses function: what is it that I see through these eyes? What is it that I choose to communicate through my lips? And what is it that I wish to absorb from the information coming to me through my ears? I, the being of light, the eternal soul and the creator; I, this point of infinitesimal energy, am the master.

Becoming aware of this, I am able to send out light and life throughout this physical body, and use this body for that which is constructive... that which is filled with goodness.

PART 2

OPENING
TO LIFELONG
LEARNING

"Human life is very precious so we must make sure that
we enjoy every moment of every day of our life.
They say life is a song, you must sing it. Life is a story, you
must write it. Life is a puzzle, you must solve it. Life is a
challenge, you must face it. Life is an entertainment you must
enjoy it. Every moment of every day of your life."

One of the most positive aspects of today's world is the transformational curve we are on. There has been a shift in consciousness. Many people are exploring a holistic approach to life and discovering the values that are truly important to them, including the concept of lifelong learning.

In the last chapter we recognized that spiritual knowledge is an essential element in the awakening of wisdom (in order to prepare the field within and to germinate the seed). But in order to continue that journey toward greater wisdom, it is no longer enough to have the *desire* to know, although of course that is important. In order to keep growing and learning, there has to be humility. The opposite of humility is ego, and ego blocks human development and inner growth.

Lifelong learning is an attitude that equips us with the irrepressible impulse to seek greater awareness – to have the openness to learn that comes from knowing there is always more to understand and discover. It is the ego that decides it doesn't need to know any more and cuts off avenues of learning. What's more, the ego is always sure that it is always right! When ego gets in the way, we can't be honest with ourselves because we can no longer access our inner wisdom. The ego, with all the manifestations of its arrogance, blocks our wisdom. How do we remove this internal blockage? Through humility; it is this quality that keeps the learning process alive throughout life, ensuring that the seedling of wisdom can continue to thrive.

The word "attitude" links back to the Latin words *aptitudo* and *aptus* – "fitness" and "fit". In humility, our attitude – our "fit position" – is one of openness and learning. With that attitude, we take responsibility for our thoughts and actions and their consequences. We are able to see what more we need to do to make things better within ourselves and also to make things better in a situation in the outside world or with other people. When we just blame and complain, we just create further dissatisfaction, which can have far-reaching effects. It then becomes almost impossible to put things right in any way because we have avoided accepting our part in the situation. But with humility also comes an acceptance, which allows the mind to be peaceful and open. Then we will have the wisdom to know what needs to be done and how to make things better.

MY OWN STORY

As I began to meditate more regularly, I began to understand that my eternal identity is not the same as my physical costume. My physical body is simply an instrument that I use at this moment, for a little while. Then I found that I wanted to find out more about the being that is actually operating this physical instrument.

Sitting in the presence of God in meditation, I felt my own innate wisdom flourish. God's light showed me the way to access the light of wisdom from within – and then I realized the vastness of the Ocean of knowledge; and with humility I appreciated quite how much I needed to learn and to grow.

With humility, I found that the wisdom of the self began to grow gently. God, my Supreme Teacher, nurtured and sustained this tiny seedling so that wisdom could flourish and blossom to maturity. The Sun of knowledge gave me the light and warmth needed to sustain that wisdom. My Teacher guides me still, gently allowing me to understand how to use my mind, and how to use the resources that I possess. As I maintain my relationship with the Supreme Teacher, I am filled with wisdom and I move towards truth.

OPENING YOURSELF TO LEARNING

To experiment and see how easy it is to switch off your ego and discover the honest inner wisdom that is deep inside you, try the following guided meditation. Experimenting with these exercises, one is able to discover the sweetness and the beauty that lies in knowing the self. The more you know yourself, the more you become able to maintain the awareness of your true identity and move away from all the different compartments and limitations that you previously imposed on yourself. The image that we generally have of ourselves is a fairly negative one, but that is simply because we don't know who we are, and so we allow external influences to restrict our thinking, put us into boxes, and create bondage, and then we feel the pain of that bondage. So put all this aside and start learning more about your true self with this exercise.

MEDITATION

I sit quietly... my thoughts focus in the centre of my forehead. I journey into my own inner world – and then I discover a whole world within my own being. I am the eternal being of light, and within myself I have the capacity to choose whichever type of thought I want to create.

For a few moments, I want to direct my thoughts into the consciousness of eternity... the awareness of truth. Who am I? I know that this body was created at a specific time. It has a beginning... it has a fixed lifespan... and so, at some point of time, later or sooner, the time span will run out and this body will finish. But I, the being of light, am eternal. I existed before this body was shaped... and I will continue to exist after this body finishes. I exist beyond the limits of time and space. I, the being of light, have a form that is infinitesimal... just a point; everything contained within a point. I, the point of light, am immortal.

In this awareness of eternity – of going beyond the limits of time and distance – I am able to have a glimpse of truth: that which is reality... that which is unchangeable... that which is the constant anchor of the universe. I stay in this awareness of I, the being of light, and touch truth and wisdom itself.

PART 3

GROWING
IN THE LIGHT

*"As I let go of ego and let in humility and love,
I keep myself open to learning, then I absorb the
wisdom that God blesses me with and the wisdom
becomes the guiding light for my life."*

So often life gets caught up in such a frantic whirlwind that we don't take a moment to pause and reflect and check in which direction life is heading. The path of meditation encourages us to do this. It forces us to stop for a while and say, "Yes, my life is important, it is valuable." In this chapter we look at ways to create the space in which to sit quietly and ask, "What is the purpose of my life and is the path that I am following actually going to take me there?" The danger of not doing this is not growing into our true wisdom. We could rush around frantically and yet never arrive at our destination unless we ascertain that the path we are following is actually going to take us there. Or perhaps, we haven't even asked ourselves what our destination truly is? Meditation means spending a little time sitting quietly in solitude, in silence within, reflecting, understanding ourselves; knowing what we want and finding out how to achieve it. Meditation is a method of liberation – of becoming free from the false impositions we have created for ourselves and which have been imposed upon us by the outside world. Meditation shows us that perfection is possible, goodness is possible, truth is possible and wisdom is possible. But none of these attributes will come about if we just sit and dream about them. Thoughts and dreams are the basis, but at some point there has to be a translation into practical life and action so that vision and dream can be realized. And so meditation and action are very closely linked. One influences the other continually.

Having had a glimpse of the identity of our true self, when it's time to leave our little corner of meditation and move into the world outside, we must learn to maintain the awareness of being a point of light: using the physical instrument of our eyes to look out into the world; using our lips to express thoughts and ideas to communicate with others. We can then be the master; listening to the information we receive, but deciding for ourselves what has value, what will enhance our awareness, which facts we should retain and what information to communicate. Also we are then able to filter out information that will pollute the mind or corrupt feelings, so that we maintain the integrity of our experience of eternal consciousness. Both things are aligned: we must relish the time we spend in silence, experiencing the eternity of the self, but then use this awareness in our day-to-day activity. If through the day we maintain this awareness, then whenever there is a moment at which actions can finish, we can turn inward and come to an awareness of peace – and then express that peace and wisdom through the work we do during the day.

Sometimes in a life that is constantly busy we ask ourselves the question, "But how can I find the time to meditate and stay aware?" We are so caught up in the mundane everyday tasks needed to fulfil our responsibilities. And it is true, our responsibilities are time consuming and they are important. However, we can still make time to grow. Let us look at a very simple day's routine. There are certain number of hours I need to devote to myself to maintain this precious vehicle – this body of mine. I need to cook for it, I need to feed it, I need to bathe it and I need to rest it. All these are my responsibilities. Nobody else can sleep for me or eat for me! I have to do all this myself. Secondly, there are responsibilities I have that concern others. When I work at my job it is not only for myself but it is also for the ones that I love or my family – the ones whom I am close to. So there are certain demands on us at that level, too. Thirdly, sometimes we choose to ignore this and yet it is a factor of consideration for everyone – we have responsibilities toward the world. Although we might not have a personal relationship with those around us in our community or society, still there is a relationship. It might not be of an intimate nature but there is an interconnectedness nonetheless. And so we do have a connection with others and a responsibility towards the world at large.

MY OWN STORY

When my own wisdom first began to awaken, my experience was of an energy that came from outside myself, an energy that was God's light and God's love. At first, I simply accepted the existence of the Supreme but, over time, I started to practise meditation, and in this way I allowed myself to be influenced by the vibrations of divine light and love.

There are, of course, many different meditation practices, but, for me, meditation is the method by which I expose myself to God's presence and allow His light and love to reach and enlighten me. When I do this – that is, when I spend time consciously allowing divine light to reach me – the wisdom within my soul is able to quicken and emerge, just as a seed sprouts into life in the warm light of the sun.

At that moment, what is knowledge is no longer just knowledge; it truly becomes wisdom. It is a combination of the knowledge I have learned and made sense of, and an exposure to God's great understanding light. The two work together, and the practical "proof" I am given of my developing wisdom is a deep certainty that I am moving in the right direction. The exposure to God's light through meditation provides me with the experience of my innate goodness and completeness, and my fleeting experiences of this perfect state serve as a blueprint for my own inner perfection.

We start to move in the right direction when we take the practical steps that allow us to reach a destination of inner perfection and completeness. In my own life, I was watching the experience of God's love and light transform my daily patterns of behaviour and relations with others – I was becoming more and more true to that blueprint of inner perfection.

MAKING TIME FOR YOURSELF TO GROW

There often doesn't seem to be time for meditation or for applying the lessons you learn in meditation to help others grow, so let's see what we can do with the time you do have. For example, the time that you spend caring for your own bodily needs. This can either be dictated by ego, greed or attachment – or you could come back to the awareness of the eternal spirit of the Soul and in that consciousness recognize that your body is a precious instrument, a gift from God, and deserves to be treated with respect. You can care for your body in the awareness that it isn't your property. You did not create it. It has come to you as a gift from God. In this awareness, the care and attention, the nurture and sustenance that you give this physical body will be one that is filled with divine love and respect. Take care of your body and service it properly, knowing that it has a very valuable task to perform. It has many things to do that are important and so you must care for it with proper attention and as you do all of this, all of this will give you a feeling of coming closer to God, and of coming closer to your own state of perfection. Every action will be filled with grace, divinity and purity – with wisdom.

So it is too, in terms of your interaction with responsibilities for others. The same task can be menial or highly uplifting. A classic story about this concerns a man building a church; in fact, there were a number of men on the building site, and an interviewer went around asking each one of them what it was they were doing. The first person replied. "I am building a wall." That was as far as his consciousness took him – which was fine; he was working with honesty and integrity, but his vision saw only the wall. Another builder said, "I am building a church"; this person had a vision which was a little broader in its perspective. He was seeing not just the wall, but something greater. The wall was to be part of a church, which was going to be powerful and beautiful. And so his attitude toward his work was filled with a different sense of awareness and intoxication; he was involved in a task that was going to produce something very beautiful. The interviewer approached another person. Same building site, same task – brick upon brick – but this individual said, "I am building something for God to be glorified." This was another vision with another consciousness – and one can imagine the quality that this builder put into his work. One can also imagine the feelings he received out of his work. And so it is with the bread and butter you earn, the job you do, the livelihood you work in – it can be either something which is dull, boring and mundane, or you can stand back a little and understand its relevance and its significance within the cosmic scheme of things.

Now let's consider your spare time, or free time. How many hours of the day do you spend watching television? How many hours a day do you lose track of? Where does time disappear? Let us look at a very simple calculation. Say you need eight hours a day for yourself, taking in all the responsibilities that you have for the upkeep of this physical instrument of yours. And perhaps you work for eight hours – eight of your hours you spend fulfilling your responsibility to others. That still leaves eight hours. What happened to them? Can you keep track of them? Well, you could spend those eight hours in spiritual study to enhance your own innate wisdom and grow and progress. You could spend that time in meditation to develop your inner potential and resources, and you could spend that time taking the lessons you learn in study and meditation and using them to serve others and give them happiness. Sharing the gifts God has given you means that others can grow also.

MEDITATION

I sit quietly; I turn inward. I visualize the point of light – the source of energy that I am. I am located in the centre of my forehead. I am a being of light.

In this awareness, rays of light extend into my physical body, and the light soothes and heals and energizes my entire physical system. My body becomes calm and relaxes... all the tension melts away, and the body becomes quiet and peaceful. And now, my mind becomes free to go into the depth of the inner being. Already, the speed of my thoughts has slowed down, and now I choose not to let my thoughts be distracted by the physical body; not to look at the scenes outside, nor to listen to the sounds outside, but to focus on that which is within my own inner being. I can feel peace within myself.

I discover I am peace. Peace isn't something outside of me... peace is within me. I can savour the sweetness of the feeling of peace. Peace is my own natural quality. This is how I used to be; and now that I know this, I am this and I can be this whenever I choose. In this awareness of peace, the vibrations of peace extend into my entire physical system, and my body returns to a state of harmony... a state of good health. Vibrations of peace spread out into the room, and from this room out into the world... and with every thought of peace, I make a contribution towards peace in the world.

PART 4

CREATING THE PERFECT BALANCE

"Ensure that every single part of the tree stays connected with the Seed, stays connected to the roots. Out of the Seed emerge the roots, and then a tiny little seedling, but then out of that very small start emerges the tree with a strong foundation, a trunk, very powerful stable branches and a myriad of leaves. When one stands back and looks at this huge tree one can appreciate beauty, strength, fullness, and most of all perfect symmetry and perfect harmony."

Traditionally, in India, when people speak of knowledge, they use the masculine form as a symbol, and when they speak of wisdom, the symbol used is the female form. In my understanding, however, the soul is both masculine and feminine, and the possibility is that each and every human soul can develop its masculine and feminine sides equally and so come to a sense of completeness and wholeness within itself.

The masculine approach to knowledge is very much connected with information, logic and reason – elements associated with the left side of the brain. The masculine, left-brain approach dominates the scientific world, in which concepts have to be rigorously proven. The feminine approach to wisdom is instead connected with intuition and creative solutions. This feminine, right-brain approach has traditionally been connected with the world of spirituality, where it is all-but impossible to prove anything through statistics and other measurable properties.

So, if we wish to allow that wisdom – which is within our own being whether we are men or women – to emerge, then we need to develop and support the right-brain principle in our day-to-day life. We can encourage the growth of this spiritual dimension of ourselves through meditation – the insights we receive through meditation allow us to gain access to and start to express our innate wisdom. Once we access this quality, we can become divine – that is, irrespective of whether the body we inhabit is male or female, we can develop a perfect balance of all the positive attributes of masculinity and femininity.

MY OWN STORY

I feel that I have a relationship with balance. There is constant change taking place – within my inner consciousness, in the body in which I live, and also in the world of matter around me. When I try to observe the changes that are happening, the easiest way to describe the changes are perhaps to think of them as a 'cycle'.

One of the things we observe from a very early age are the cycles of day and night: when the sun shines we come to understand that the sun will set and that night will gradually come, and even if we wake in the middle of the night and it's pitch dark, we know that there will be light; that the sun will rise again. A little later in life, we begin to understand the cycle of the seasons. We see that it is winter, when there seems to be no life, and yet even at that moment we have hope. We know that in a few weeks, or a few months, the first signs of spring will show, and when spring comes, hope comes into our hearts again and we know that the little buds that are emerging will blossom forth until everything is beautifully fresh, fertile and alive again.

Having experienced the joy of springtime, seeing everything blossom and flourish, by the time it gets round to the summer things are not so bright as they were and we know that already, even at the very peak of summer, there is already a turning point and after that powerful blossoming will come a period of gradual decay and wilting. By autumn we are aware that a major change has taken place. We can see how the leaves have changed in colour and gradually we expect that they will fall off and that winter will return once more. The season's cycle is something we actually learn to appreciate and enjoy. Each season brings a particular beauty and special fruits to look forward to.

The same thing applies in human life – a child takes birth, passes through adolescence, reaches maturity and from then on comes a gradual slowing of all the processes, approaching old age; then we know that there will shortly be a departure. But we don't always connect that departure with an arrival; another birth. So in human life we go through a cycle, too.

There are cycles all around us – even in terms of the economy, experts can predict ascent and decline; they understand how these energies work. In fact, it is rare to see anything happen in the form of a straight line. Straight lines seem to be human-generated; we have created them artificially. Nature by itself just doesn't have a straight line; everything is actually part of a curve or a cyclical pattern. But we still like to think of time as being linear. We think that human civilization and knowledge started at a particular point and has gradually been evolving and moving forward – I wonder whether we actually ever question whether it is going to peak at some point or what will happen beyond the peak? Well, let's look at that theory further. If I continue to extend a straight line further and further and further – if I extend a straight line to infinity, where would I arrive? I would probably come back to the starting point, and I would find that I have been through a circle, a cycle. In terms of spiritual consciousness, one begins to see time in this way; with no beginning or end point. Most of the major religions of the world have used the word "eternal" to describe the spirit. If I try to think of a way to describe eternity in the form of a diagram, the only way that I can think of it is to describe a circle.

CREATING YOUR OWN BALANCE

Spiritual consciousness makes us aware of things moving in cycles. One of the very first aspects of spirituality, knowing the self, means not only knowing your present state of consciousness – whether you think of it as masculine and analytical or feminine and intuitive – but actually being able to stand back, become detached and able to see the self in the awareness of eternity. When you're willing to step away from the consciousness of matter, step away from the body and step back a little, then in that consciousness you begin to have a tiny glimpse of eternal consciousness. It's only through this very personal awareness and feeling of eternal consciousness that you're then able to look at the world around you and the concept of time and become able to see time as a cycle. Within the soul is a part that is recorded, which is why at times you intuitively know what you are going to say to me, or intuitively I know what is around the next corner. It's as if there is an awareness recorded within the self. Sometimes, especially when we hear spiritual teachings, we have a sense of having heard all of this before, of it being pre-recorded within the self. Someone has just come along and been a stimulus, awakening that consciousness. So as you listen it doesn't feel like listening to new information, it's as if you are listening to things that you know already, knowledge that you have heard before, facts that perhaps you intuited previously but were not able to formulate in words. Within this eternal being that you are is this amazing storehouse of information – everything is already recorded within the self and the insight you gain through meditation and spiritual study will open it up to you.

MEDITATION

I sit comfortably, and let the body relax... and as I let all the tension of the body fall away, I focus my thoughts in the centre of my forehead. I am a being of light – a spiritual being. And in this awareness I move away from the limits of matter; I, the eternal being, move into a dimension of light... and in this world of light I look at the world of matter and I can see a world in which there are beginnings and endings. But in this dimension of light there is only infinity – there is no beginning, there is no end. I find myself in a dimension of infinite space... a world that is eternal. My mind begins to be aware of the vastness of eternity...

In this experience I know that I too have no beginning and no end... I am eternal. I carry within myself eternal peace, light and love.

And from this moment of eternity, I come back into the consciousness of matter... into the awareness of my own physical body and the world around me. And I see the reality of this world of time and space, but I keep this feeling of the eternal soul – beyond time... beyond space...

PART 5

NURTURING THE CHILD WITHIN

"The first step in terms of recognizing my own value is to be able to see myself as a child of God, to stabilise myself in that awareness and to begin to appreciate who I am and what it is that God is making me and has given me already. Chant this mantra everyday – 'I love and value myself'."

In adult-child relationships, if the culture in the family home, or later on at school, is one of discipline and harshness or forceful correction, then a child is not allowed to develop in a positive way; that child's potential can not be properly expressed.

Teachers who have been working with positive values in education have produced impressive results. If we create a culture in which we all respect these values – values such as encouragement, optimism, honesty, truth and goodness – the results are dramatic. Not only in terms of academic excellence, but in the development of character and the atmosphere of the school and the children's own homes.

So we now have a lot of evidence that when an environment is filled with acceptance and positive encouragement, then whatever is good within a child will be expressed and developed in the right way. Let us now think about the child within each of us – how can we best be responsible for the care and nurture of that child? Thinking in this way can bring us back to a state of balance so that wisdom then guides the way in which we live. We have plenty of "child-care" information out there in the world, and it is very useful, but the real guidance we need comes through wisdom.

When thinking about the notion of nurturing our inner child with acceptance and positivity, it's useful to start by asking, "Who am I?" What is the image we have of ourselves? Very often when we introduce ourselves we mention nationality, gender, age, profession, the colour of our eyes, the colour of our hair, the colour of our skin. If we have all this information about a person, how well are we able to know him or her? All these details are valuable, but in fact they provide no information whatsoever about the true identity of that individual – and if under some misunderstanding we think they do, it leads to many disappointments.

For example, if my perception of a human being is coloured by their nationality or gender, I'll run into many obstacles in my relationship with them because preconceived notions influence my attitude towards them. These notions are not truly based on reality. It would be like saying that there is a whole nation that possesses one particular characteristic or another, and yet we know that every family is highly individual and no one family shares the same characteristics. Every member of the family is unique and different, too – so how can all the members of one race or one nation be the same? Every human being is individual and unique.

So what is your identity? Are you your profession? This question has become part of our modern crisis. If I say I'm an engineer, what happens if I'm made redundant? Do I have an identity that exists beyond being an engineer? The same question crops up if I define myself in terms of my relationship with another person. For example, saying "I am a mother" can provide me with a wonderful sense of security while my child is young and needs me and sees me as his mother. But from the moment that child wishes to exert his own authority and exercise his own individuality – wants to be a human being in his own right – which of course he must do, then I am no longer just a mother. If my consciousness revolves around this one relationship, I face a crisis. Yet in fact I exist as a very valuable and precious human being, irrespective of the roles I play and irrespective of the responsibilities and tasks I take on.

MY OWN STORY

So who am I? Within the space of twenty-four hours – or for however many hours I maintain consciousness – I play a number of different roles. At one moment I'm a friend, at another moment I'm a teacher, and at another moment still I'm a dishwasher or a cleaner. All of these roles are important; each one is a different channel through which I can express aspects of my own being. The roles that I have mentioned are perhaps not so glamorous. Maybe there are more exiting roles that I play. Maybe I'm also a business person, maybe I'm a writer or an artist. There can be a thousand and one different roles I play. All these roles are extensions of my own inner being; my personality. I use different facets of my personality to express myself through these different channels. We are all well accustomed to this; a problem arises only if I lock myself in a specific role at the expense of the other roles or I deny the existence of my full personality because one role becomes dominant and blocks out other aspects. I then become stagnant, and because I'm not a complete rounded personality, other people have difficulties in their relationships with me. Part of knowing myself is to know that within I, the inner being, is a whole world of experience and I can choose which role to play at the time that is appropriate and in a way that is appropriate. I can express aspects of my personality in each of these different roles. I'm therefore also able to fulfil my responsibilities in each of these roles. It means that I have to learn to distance myself from my role – from my responsibility – and see what lies within my inner being. The inner being actually has a separate identity to all the factors associated with the physical form.

I, the inner being, am a being of light. I, the inner being, exist eternally; I existed even before this body was shaped; I existed before I created that particular role. I have not been created by the role; I have created that role. When I understand this, then my value doesn't depend on either my role, my responsibility, or the way in which others perceive my role and responsibility. I exist as a human being with dignity, with value and with self-respect. I bring these qualities to bear on the role that I then play. In the awareness of my eternal identity, I play my role and I do so with the best of my ability – and yet I'm not locked into it, I'm not in a state of bondage to my role, and therefore I am able to play it exceedingly well. I'm also able to listen and offer praise or criticism with an inner sense of detachment – I am able to retain mastery and control over my emotions. I don't allow myself to become the puppet of other people, so there is no manipulation. I maintain the integrity of my own independence and freedom.

NURTURING YOUR INNER CHILD

So the best way to nurture who you really are is to recognize your own eternal self. You can do this most easily through meditation. As you begin to know yourself in terms of eternity, you begin to respect and love this inner child. You see yourself with esteem and then your vision of others takes on the same quality. With knowledge of your wise self, you see every human being irrespective of the colour of their skin, of the religion they belong to, of their age or gender. You become able to see each human being as the eternal being with whom you have an eternal connection. If you regard them in terms of their role in life or connection to another person, you can only make a temporary connection with them, because we only play a specific role with another human being for a limited period of time. But by stepping out of the consciousness of your physical costume, and the limited bondages that it imposes, you step into eternity. Then you can look around and become aware of your eternal connection with every human being. A deep sense of brotherhood comes to your awareness – a realization of the connection we have with each other through time, for all eternity.

In this awareness of your eternal state you can nurture your inner child by recognizing two sides of your being. You can see the positive, identifing goodness, talent and specialities without ego influencing your thoughts. In the confidence and security of your own goodness you also have the courage to look at the other side – the picture that isn't quite as beautiful. You are able to identify the flaws, the stains, the weaknesses and the defects within your own characteristics – and to simply acknowledge them, accepting that these are part of your being at the moment. Nurturing your inner child means offering yourself acceptance and positivity. Having the awareness of eternity allows you to be gentle with your weaknesses. You can appreciate that this negative patch is just that – a phase that you happen to be passing through. These negative traits are not your original traits; they're not your eternal traits. You've had them for just a short period in the present moment. What you can do is gently amend, alter and adjust, so that you deal with these negative aspects and transform them. In the awareness of the eternal self you know that in your original state there is nothing but peace, love, truth, wisdom and purity. In that awareness you have the power and the capacity to be able to deal with the negativity that has revealed itself at the present time.

Not only can you acknowledge this for yourself – you can use the same positive vision to look at others. Perhaps, at the present time, they too have defects and weaknesses, yet these too are only temporary. They are not the eternal qualities of the eternal being. Stable in the vision of your own eternity, you can see others with that eternal vision and see the truth within that other soul, you will be able to see the speciality of that soul and the goodness of that soul. In a very genuine way a brotherhood of love and respect can be created once more.

In meditation you can practise this awareness of eternal consciousness, but before and after meditation it is equally important to maintain this positive vision of eternity both to raise your own inner child well and to nurture others. It's very simple. As you travel through your day just be aware that the soul is using this body to walk, the soul is using these physical eyes to see, and the soul is using these lips to communicate. Simply issue this gentle reminder to the self again and again.

MEDITATION

Sitting quietly, allowing the body to relax and become quiet, so that there are no distractions, I begin my inner journey. Focusing on the centre of my forehead I visualize a point of light. This is who I truly am. The body is my instrument and I, the master of this body, am the being of light. I can feel a sense of separation.

From this space in the centre of my forehead, I acknowledge my responsibility to this valuable instrument and I send out rays of light... I send rays of peace. And now I turn deep inside this point of light. I can see the waves on the screen of my mind. I allow them to slow down, and I pick up one thought – I am light. I let myself feel within this point of light... this eternal consciousness... there is peace. Peace, totally natural, belonging to me, within me. Peace, so deep, so rich that I know it is my own natural state of being.

I am light... I am peace. My thoughts come back to the awareness of my physical body and my present surroundings, but I keep this consciousness.

PART 6

GROWING IN
SELF-BELIEF

"The reason that I'm not able to value myself is because I don't know myself well enough and this is why I said that we have information of the world outside but yet we don't often seek the information about the world inside. A spiritual journey means to be able to travel inward and understand what is going on within my own inner being. The more I know myself, the more I'm able to love myself. Without knowing myself it's not possible to love myself."

---◆---

Just as we can apply positive values to the education of children and an equally positive attitude to all the friends, family and colleagues with whom we interact, so we can bring the equivalent of all this positivity to ourselves, enriching that inner space in which we planted our seed of wisdom. By having meaningful conversations with ourselves that are considered, reflective and optimistic, the seed of wisdom begins to sprout, put out leaves and slowly but surely grow into a sapling. As our positive words fill us with self-esteem, we can watch our own tree of wisdom flourish.

To have doubts about ourselves reveals a lack of wisdom. Doubt disturbs us and makes us fluctuate so that we lose our self-belief. But even at this point, if we can stop and recall the knowledge we had of our innate perfection – when we became aware in meditation of our inner light and love – we can then begin to move again in the right direction. And the more we remember the joy and the longing to learn we felt, the more our faith and self-belief will strengthen to give us an unshakeable and immovable self-respect.

Perhaps one of the main reasons why we don't have self-esteem is our lack of self-knowledge. We are bombarded on all sides by knowledge and information about the world outside us, and of course it is very valuable. We've been able to achieve many, many things as a result. However, we still lack information about the world inside us. A spiritual journey means travelling inward to understand what is going on within our own inner being. The more we know about ourselves, the more we become able to love ourselves. Without knowing yourself, it's not possible to love yourself.

So when we look at ourselves inside, what do we see? First, of course, we are aware of the mind – the power or ability to create thoughts – and generally we see that it is in a state of upheaval! We have no idea where our thoughts are coming from, and even less idea of where those thoughts are leading to – at any moment our thoughts are scattered in a dozen different directions. In today's world we all complain about lack of concentration – the mind seems to flicker like a butterfly from one subject to another without being able to understand or experience the depth of anything. When we look inside ourselves, we may experience this as an almost aggressive state, like a stormy sea. But once we get to know our inner self better, we begin with the faith that deep within ourselves is a still point of peace – a point of stability within the inner being – and by getting in touch with this place, we can learn to still those stormy thoughts and descend deep below the superficial factors that are causing us such distraction. These could be thoughts about the body, thoughts about other people, or thoughts about material possessions and other external things. If we can let the mind become quiet, we can touch in with that inner peace deep within our being.

And from this state of inner peace and awareness we can begin to understand why we haven't been able value ourselves or have respect for ourselves. We see that within our own inner being we have a conscience. Ah, now we begin to see what has been happening. Whenever that conscience spoke we were ignoring it. We just went ahead and did other things, or, when we heard the soft, quiet voice of the conscience, we agreed that it was correct and yet lacked the power, or capacity, to be able to implement what it was suggesting. And so that conscience stopped speaking; instead of being our friend, it became silent and just looked on, watching and observing. Because of this, we were not able to accept its help or count on its support and over months and even years we gradually lost any value for ourselves – maybe you even actually forgot your own self. At the point that we moved away from understanding the conscience and realizing the truth, life went off in a different direction, and so we stopped valuing ourselves. So perhaps the most important way to regain your own value, your own inner dignity and respect for yourself, is to come back to the point of truth. And truth begins within your mind and within your own conscience. When your world is simply materialistic, lacking an awareness of the spiritual dimension, it's difficult to understand the truth – and inner wisdom then withers and dies.

MY OWN STORY

I used to compare myself a little with other people, thinking that my spiritual progress would be helped by doing so. But instead I became a little disheartened and my heart seemed to shrink. Then I turned my attention inward and the thought came to me that each one of us has his or her own speciality and own uniqueness – so no one of us can compare ourselve to any other person. Immediately, I felt so light and free to be myself and to see myself as valuable. I realized that out of all the millions of souls in the world, no one is the same as me. Each one of us is so very special.

Turning inward and discovering myself, I realized that I had become a stranger to myself. I had forgotten myself, and so I had not been able to love myself; and then, in discovering myself again, I begin to make friends with myself. I started to acknowledge the value of my own existence; the beauty of my own being – and with this recognition I once more begin to love myself and respect myself. In the flowering of this inner strength I returned to that state of dignity once more.

GROW YOUR OWN SELF-BELIEF

The world of matter creates many distractions, from possessiveness to desires and attachments. Perhaps it is these last two factors – desires and attachments – that most cause you to move away from your own inner state of self-esteem. If you place value on things outside yourself – on possessions – you lose sense of your own value. And if you place your values in the hands of others, you become dependent, or attached. Of course in that state of dependency, it's not possible to have value for your self and self-esteem. So desires and attachments are the things you have to deal with in order to grow wiser. Then you gain your independence again, and with that grows dignity and the ability to stand freely on your own two feet.

As you understand all these things, the confusion begins to lift, things become clear and you begin to know yourself and see what it is you need to do. That aspect within your own inner being – the innate wisdom connected with your intellect – begins to open and you see yourself as a spiritual being. Knowing your spiritual identity, power begins to grow within, clarity develops and, as a result of this, the conscience becomes strong and clear, and you are able to start disciplining the mind; not suppressing other thoughts, but simply training the mind to think in the right way. As you create the right thoughts based on truth, you begin to perform actions based on truth. The words you speak are, of course, an expression of the things you have been thinking. Those too, then, are based on truth. Words and actions are in alignment with each other. Inside and outside are the same; there is a transparency and honesty. As you see life moving in this direction you become able to hold your head high, and to value and respect yourself. Stable in the security of your own awareness, you are able to give respect to others, too. Perhaps in the past you sought respect from others first before giving it back. Maybe you thought, "Well they didn't give me respect so why should I give them respect?" But once your own inner world has been put right and you are able to see yourself with a new vision of love and respect, then you are able to start giving. And if you are able to give respect to you... and you... and you, then at some point cause and effect – action and reaction – is such that the same respect will be returned to you, further building your self-esteem. If it is not, no matter what others have done, you feel able to continually show respect to them. So the starting point is knowing yourself, the next step is to respect yourself, but, further than that, you should also be able to love yourself. When you begin to respect yourself because your life is now based on truth, other beautiful things start to happen and your mind becomes calm and peaceful instead of stormy and aggressive.

A life based on truth means having a guarantee that things are going to move in the right way always; your mind is liberated from fear, anxiety and worry; and now you know that only good things can happen and, whatever may happen, the power of truth will give you the strength to surmount all obstacles. Based on this awareness of total stability and security, you can look within yourself and find not only peace, but contentment, joy, purity and strength. You are able to see all the goodness stored within the soul. In the original state there is goodness within the soul, and this state of self-esteem now gives you a picture of what that goodness really is. Seeing the inner beauty of the self, the soul begins to love itself, and in this experience of love for the self the heart is able to grow. The barriers that existed before all melt away and there is open space. Not only do you now love yourself, but you are able to see others with this vision of love because you are no longer seeking to take from others; instead an energy is flowing and reaching out to others. You can share love and as that love is shared and distributed of course it turns around and comes back to you. So wherever you go, you find yourself surrounded by love. A state of fear attracts negative energy from others, but in the state of love only love comes back to you, nothing else.

Within relationships, this state of self-esteem means that now you are able to give instead of take. But also it means that now you can begin to co-operate with others. Generally, when there is fear because of insecurity, we either have to prove ourselves to be superior or enter into competition with others and sometimes feel inferior. It's not possible to work together. Ego is one of the chief enemies of creativity and co-operation, and when we lack knowledge of the self and live in a state of ignorance, ego predominates. Ego is connected with physical consciousness of the body and an arrogance that encourages us to prove that we are right and better than others; this prevents co-operation. But in a state of inner dignity and self-esteem – when you are able to see and value others and their specialities and talents – you are able to come together with others without needing to prove anything, without any ego. And in that state, when our energies combine in a constructive way, things are more powerful and more beautiful than their individual parts emerge; we come together with a creative energy that produces things of great beauty and strength.

In relationships, too, when there is the power of co-operation, of coming together, a trust grows between us. We know that we can rely on each other; we know that we are going to be able to move together in the same direction. Things that you could not achieve on your own become possible. Impossible dreams become a reality.

Self-esteem means balance within the self but also balance in relationships. When there is balance in relationships then at times I can share something but at times you share also. Think about a world in which each one of us is not only independent, but also interdependent. The starting point is to set yourself free by nurturing your self-esteem. In a state of dependency, which is the state without self-esteem, it's not possible to come together with creative energies, but self-esteem sets us free and allows us to work with others, play with others, love others and join forces with others to move toward a better future for all of us together.

MEDITATION

Sitting quietly, I move my thoughts away from my own body, human beings and possessions, and I come back to my spiritual identity – the true identity of the self – and I find that point of peace within me. And as I look at myself in the state of peace, I understand that my conscience has to be activated.

Knowing myself as a spiritual being gives new life to the conscience, so that it awakens... and in this state of awareness, with my conscience awake and clear, strength grows and I become able to discern truth. In this state of peace and stability, not only do I understand truth, I have the capacity to follow the path of truth within my thoughts, truth within my words, truth within my actions... truth.

As a silent, detached observer of myself, I see the darkness of ignorance leave me. I see the light of truth grow... and as truth returns to my inner being, I am able to have regard for myself... and with this power of truth and respect I am freed. No more dependencies... no more desires... no more attachments. Truth is within my own inner being... purity is my original state of being; in my original state I am pure, I am clean.

Seeing myself in this condition, I appreciate myself, I love myself and joy springs within my heart. I return to my own original state of goodness. I know I am a unique and valuable being. Keeping this awareness, I come back to the awareness of my role in life, but I bring back this inner dignity and self-esteem to guide me in the roles that I play.

PART 7

OVERCOMING CRITICISM

"If there are teachings, instructions or corrections to be given, always give them with a lot of love, and no trace of anger."

Wisdom needs an inner space – a field – in order for its seed and its saplings to flourish. Put poison onto the earth in that field and the seed will be destroyed, but supplement the ground with all the good things that nourish a little seed of wisdom and you give it a good chance of growing healthy, strong and fast – the tree it grows into will be far more beautiful than if the seed were neglected. This is a reality. If we poison the field of our minds, then whatever wisdom was beginning to grow is gone; it is killed. Which poison most destroys the human mind? Criticism. And so this chapter offers ways to overcome that all-too-common human urge.

How do we overcome the urge to criticize? I find one of the best ways is to develop another skill, or human power – the ability to let go. Each day of our lives carries a thousand different experiences. Perhaps even a million different experiences! And we have to find a way of keeping hold of the experiences that are useful – the things that help us to learn and grow – and letting go of those that are damaging for our minds. We have to learn to sort out and separate, pack up and keep together those skills we will need for tomorrow, but also how to settle, end and dispense with things that are no longer useful. We can access the ability to let go and to also carry forward qualities and thoughts we are going to need tomorrow through our own spiritual power.

If we lack this spiritual power, we won't be able to decide what is going to be of value – what will help those little seeds to grow – and what is not so useful; what is simply going to be a burden or even poison the soil that those seeds are rooted in. Spiritual power means firstly having the clarity with which to be able to see the valuable and the poison, and then secondly, having the power to say, "This is rubbish; this is not useful; these are chains that are holding me down, and I don't need them any more," and then to pack up and move on. We might compare this process to embarking on a physical journey; if all you can carry with you is a back-pack, you will decide what is most useful to take on your travels. When you stay at home, with more space than in a back-pack, you can spread your possessions here and there, thinking that this or that might come in handy later on; you can accumulate, and gradually those rooms become filled with so much stuff that one day you look around and say, "How did I manage to gather all this stuff together?" At that point, having to let go seems very difficult. But if you are forced into a situation where you have to choose, and select only the few essentials that fit into a back-pack, it's no problem. You prioritize and weigh up exactly what will be useful; from experience, you know what will be a heavy burden or an unnecessary distraction along the way. And so you set to one side those items that are not useful.

I am talking here not only about the physical aspect of life and possessions – although being able to let go on this level is important if you are to become a wiser person. I am talking more about inner awareness. We do not have infinite space or infinite capacity within our own consciousness. In fact, there's only a very tiny, very precious, very valuable amount of space within us – and so it is crucial that we decide what we need, what we have to keep, and what we must let go off and throw away. We don't need those memories of past pain, for instance, just as we don't need to keep a record of all the injustice that has happened to us. We don't need that negative outlook and critical stance. We don't need any of the things that cause bitterness and sorrow. Yes, we all need to learn lessons from the past – and we need to keep those lessons very clearly in mind to prevent us from acting in a similar way in the future – but the pain, the bitterness, the anger? There's definitely no place for those. When we realize how precious the space inside our head is, and how limited it is, then we have to make a choice. Do we want to fill it with good things or all this dead, negative stuff? It's easy to make the choice if it's put in this way. And at the moment we realize this, we can just let go and notice how much lighter, much happier, much more focused and more concentrated we feel.

MY OWN STORY

On one occasion in the past, after much thought had confirmed to me that I was right, I explained to someone who was my senior that a situation was wrong. She did not accept my view. I knew this senior figure was very sensible and so this left me confused, "I'm right," I thought, "and she's very sensible but she's just not understanding me – and I think I'm being as clear as I possibly can be. What's going on?" I decided not to force the point, but instead to go into my inner space of silence. When I did become silent, my senior explained, "Of course I can see; how could I not see? But what is it that I must acknowledge and support? Am I going to support that negative view – your negative stance – or am I going to support the positive within the situation and within the individual, so that they can be empowered to move on? I'm not going to support negative stories, even if they are right."

She was correct, of course. It is very easy to be critical, because all of us feel we are intelligent and that we understand. Yet every time we are critical of someone, we are poisoning our relationship with that person. We are poisoning the atmosphere, too. But most dangerous of all, we are poisoning our own minds. And when we poison our minds, we destroy the seed of wisdom, maybe even before it has had the chance to germinate.

Instead of being critical, we must distinguish between discerning right from wrong and criticism. The two are not the same. Indeed, discernment is very important. It's our emotional reaction and our expression of right and wrong that becomes a critical expression because the emotions of attachment and possessiveness cloud our ability to give clear guidance as to what is right or wrong. To be more discerning, we need to lay down guidelines and assert some discipline.

Let's use this as an example: suppose that teenagers are coming home later and later – in the early hours of the morning rather than during the evening – and pushing the boundaries further and further. There comes a point at which the parent needs to sit down with them and explain the rules of the house and the discipline they are expected to observe. Once the teenagers leave home, of course, the rules become their choice; but while parents are responsible, they must be in control of the discipline. It takes clarity, wisdom and love to be able to do that and stay clear of criticism. Otherwise emotion and attachment either lead parents to avoid confrontation and have a laissez-faire attitude, or else they make them become overbearing and angry, which may lead the children to rebel. So how do you develop the clarity and wisdom to be able to be discerning without being critical?

GROW YOUR OWN WISDOM

When you think of your weaknesses, it is as if you are putting a stamp on those weaknesses. If you do this, they tend to grow, and your own strength – or innate wisdom – is reduced. The same thing happens when you start looking at the weaknesses of others. It doesn't actually matter who is right and who is wrong. Every time your energy focuses on the weaknesses of another, it drains you of your inner power, and if that negative vision is translated into words so that you criticize or gossip, that's another huge drop in energy for the soul. And so negative criticism of the self, towards the past or towards other people – all of these create an energy loss.

Having understood that, why not decide to turn things around? You are responsible for your own inner world. Accepting that responsibility, start moving in the right direction. Try this very simple experiment: create good thoughts, pure thoughts, positive thoughts, noble thoughts, elevated thoughts, thoughts of goodness, thoughts of compassion, thoughts of love. Do you feel your inner strength and innate wisdom growing? And if these good thoughts are actually translated into words – words that can inspire, encourage and support or help others – then comes a wonderful influx of energy into the soul. If as a result of those good thoughts you are actually able to express this new-found energy in action, and actually do good things in life, the power of good action is such that good things not only happen externally, but strength grows within.

There are two words which are very simple and yet very old-fashioned. We don't like using them in today's world, but they are a reality. The first word is "sin" and the second "charity". Any aspect of sinful behaviour – any action connected with sin – will deplete you of your spiritual power and reduce your inner wisdom. And yet any action based on giving – on concern for others, compassion, generosity and charity – will fill you with strength. Understanding this means you can see why you lost power and clarity, or lost touch with your inner wisdom; but it also means that you know how to regain them. When you have that inner power again within your being, you are able to do good things once more, existing not only for yourself as a human individual, but to serve a higher purpose.

MEDITATION

Sitting quietly, I stop my mind from running around in many different directions and I focus it in one direction – the awareness of the eternal point of light that I am.

In this awareness of I, the eternal soul, I use my thoughts to connect with the Supreme. As I make contact with the being of light who is the Supreme, God's light... God's love... reaches me, filling me with strength. Darkness dissolves and only the light remains. In this awareness of my own original state of peace... of truth... of light, energy grows within my being. From the Supreme, light and might reach the soul. This light and might extend out into the universe... the darkness of the world finishes and we move into a world of light.

Keeping this connection with the Supreme, I come back to the awareness of my responsibilities here in the physical dimension, but now I use this inner power to guide me and keep me moving toward my destination. As I use my resources in a worthwhile way – my thoughts, my words, my actions, my time, my talents – so my inner power grows.

Every time in the past that I used my resources in a wasteful way or negative way I lost power – but now, in this awareness of light and might from the Divine, knowing what I should be doing, using all my resources well, my inner strength grows.

PART 8

ENCOURAGING POSITIVITY

"First of all I need to teach my mind to think positive. If I am able to make my mind positive then my mental reaction will be positive. The golden key is to teach myself to think positive."

———— •◆• ————

Broadly speaking, emotions fall into two main categories: positive or negative. An extremely negative emotion can give us a powerful, highly charged sensation that may feel quite exciting – but, as we learned in the previous chapter about criticism, such negativity has a poisoning and corroding effect on the wisdom that lies within the soul. If we choose to nurture a positive emotion instead, wisdom grows.

Taking time to create a link with God through meditation is not just an intellectual exercise, but very much a feeling of the heart and an emotional experience as well. If the heart is open to the experience, sometimes meditation can be emotionally very moving and positive. This is evident in many of the writings of the medieval Christian mystics, such as Saint Hildegard of Bingen or Mother Julian of Norwich. Their words of amazing wisdom and the experiences they share with us through their writing display a very beautiful, powerful and personal knowledge of divine love. My very strong sense about them is that, whereas we've thought mystics are other people belonging to the past, it's important to realize that each one of us has that capacity. In fact, each one of us today actually has the *right* – even though we might be living a family life, within a household – to be able to have the same mystical experience of God's love. This wisdom should not be thought of as separate, or only for those who choose a life of renunciation and seclusion. This wisdom does not belong to another level. Meditation automatically gives us access to all those wonderful emotions and feelings.

Meditation brings us self-knowledge, and this teaches us how to adjust our feelings, so that whereas in the past we may have reacted without thinking to a negative emotion, we have a new presence of mind and do not react. After meditation we have enough knowledge and wisdom within our consciousness to be able to tell ourselves that we don't need to react to negativity. We know how to choose not to go in that direction. We are able to convert those unhelpful feelings and emotions, transforming and sublimating states such as anger or jealousy, so that wisdom is allowed to develop. By removing the weeds from the field, we create the conditions in which the seedling of wisdom can grow strong.

Anger is the most destructive emotion for wisdom. In Raja Yoga meditation, we believe that the personality, the tendencies and the traits we carry within us are not fixed in stone but are open and adjustable. And if we can imbibe peace deeply within ourselves and allow the peace that is already naturally within us to grow, we can actually change anger, rather than suppressing it. In fact, we can transform it.

Every interaction we have with another person creates a powerful impact on us. We don't realize quite how influential we are and the impact we have on others, though from time to time we may get a glimpse of our potency – for example, if a positive word of encouragement comes at a moment when someone really needs it, it will leave an imprint on that person's heart and way of life. We may be able to notice the effect of our words on his or her life choices.

So by encouraging others, our positive contribution allows wisdom to grow in those around us; when we give happiness we remove sorrow. So let our words be empty of criticism and negativity and instead be filled with a sweetness and optimism and truth. We need to ask ourselves constantly whether our conversations are ordinary or meaningful, useful or even filled with wisdom. Do we give each other quality time in which there can be an exchange that is meaningful? This is the way to allow wisdom to flourish – in ourselves and in others.

MY OWN STORY

In my journey from the inner experience of these original qualities of the soul to that state in which they actually become power, I see that it is my relationship with God that makes the difference. In my own experience, even the development and the journey of accessing these qualities and using them in my life requires the presence of God and the influence of God. This is because there is so much negativity in the world around us; in fact, there is so much that we become influenced by it very easily. I, on my own, would find it very difficult to move constantly in the direction of peace, but if I hold myself under the canopy of protection provided by remembrance of God, and through a relationship of companionship and friendship with God, then I am able to maintain my own quality of peace in my life. But more than this; through that link with the Supreme, as I draw God's peace within myself, then it is not only *my* own original quality of peace or *my* own original quality of love – it is multiplied with God's power of peace and God's power of love. This power then extends out into the universe. I believe that it is possible to actually bring about transformation in the world and move in the direction of a world of peace and love by allowing ourselves to become channels of God's power in this way.

BECOMING MORE POSITIVE FOR YOURSELF

There are very simple ways to make sure this same kind of positivity works in your own life. One step is to maintain your own inner peace, no matter how aggravating the circumstances around you may be. Allow yourself to maintain an attitude of non-violence and peace, no matter how much the stimulus from outside may try to push you in the direction of violence. But more than that, as your own peace and wisdom multiplies with the power of God's peace and wisdom, see how the atmosphere around you is transformed and how you generate an oasis of peace that is able to touch everybody else who enters that sphere – so that they, too, are transformed. The vibrations of peace reach them and they carry away that experience of peace. Then it extends further and further, beyond just the interactions we have with each other, or beyond the immediate atmosphere that we generate. The power of vibrations is able to reach out into the universe and bring about a total transformation of the globe. This is what we all have to aim towards.

It has been said that the power of prayer is able to work miracles, and I think that this is the mechanism by which miracles can actually happen. It is interesting to see how even miracles can be understood, and the more I understand them, the more I am able to operate them and actually make them happen. So my – and your – own inner journey, from the experience of qualities and values of truth, through to the adherence to those virtues, and interaction with others using those values, creates a state in which the power of peace, the power of love, the power of truth, the power of joy and the power of purity is able to create a world based on these qualities.

Personal empowerment just for yourself alone is wonderful, but I think as we understand these secrets and empower each other,

God's power is able to transform the world. Spiritual wisdom is actually a power that is able to bring about change. Spiritual power doesn't simply work in the sense of making a dead person alive or taking away sickness on a physical level, but spiritual power is something we experiment with on a day-to-day basis in our own lives. Things that normally we wouldn't be able to tolerate, situations that would perhaps leave us confused, experiences that we wouldn't normally be able to cope with, are transformed as we develop our own wisdom. And we are able to see tangible results of this in our own lives. As we move toward a state in which these qualities are maintained on a continual basis within our lives, we become able to demonstrate both to ourselves and to those around us how spiritual wisdom can work.

The word "power" is often misunderstood. We associate it with having power over another person – and in a world which considers personal freedom as one of the most valuable experiences in life – one of our most treasured possessions – we certainly don't want to hand over power to another. The reality is that we often do this, and spiritual power firstly means being able to free ourselves from such dependency. Spiritual power doesn't mean exerting authority over others. Spiritual power means being able to keep ourselves free, or in a state of liberation: free from influence and free from bondage. We are able to become master of ourselves. An indication of our power is the ability to stand on our own feet: independent, free, willing to make choices, and able to move in the direction we want to. This is true wisdom.

MEDITATION

Sitting quietly, I set aside thoughts of my physical existence for just a few moments. The physical dimension of life is important and I need to pay attention to it, but now, just for a few moments, I set that to one side and explore the world of the spirit... the dimension of spirituality.

As I journey inward, I explore the world inside my own mind and I see thousands of strands all moving very quickly in many, many different directions. I stand back and I watch this amazing scene of energy being scattered in a thousand different ways... and now I decide to focus my energy. I pull my thoughts together and I create one positive thought... the thought of peace. I allow my mind to move slowly, creating peace. As I allow peace to flow through my mind, I begin to access the peace that is within my own being. Peace feels natural... peace feels as if it belongs to me... and I know that this is true. In my original state of being, I am peace... and in this state of peace I am able to experience the presence of God. I find myself surrounded by the Ocean of Peace.

My own inner quality of peace enables me to make contact with the Source of Peace the Ocean of Peace... and the power of peace multiplies... and the vibrations of peace extend out into the universe. As the vibrations of peace touch human souls they become peaceful and as the vibrations of peace touch the elements of matter, nature becomes peaceful... and the power of peace envelops the globe.

PART 9

CULTIVATING
DISCERNMENT

"What we call the state of detachment means you are in the water like the lotus flower, but the water does not touch the petals of the flower. There is no taking sides about anything; you are neutral. There is no partiality or prejudices, you are just detached; that is why you are not affected. It doesn't mean you are isolated. Detachment means you are very much there, observing, but you are not affected; that stage of wisdom is possible."

———— •—◆—• ————

Now as our wisdom is sprouting and putting out shoots of new growth, we must look at another potential inhibitor of growth. There is a very deep but subtle trap that blocks the growth of the wisdom of the soul. This is attachment. If, in our relationships, we look for support or depend on the support only of a human being, we tend not to trust our own innate wisdom, but instead seek confirmation from that other person. We give that person's opinion a great deal of weight. There's a difference between having a relationship with those who are wise – from them we can take help and guidance – and having a relationship with people on whom we rely for emotional support. This is a form of co-dependency, whether subtle or overt. Such dependency can invalidate our own inner understanding of what is right or true for us. And it can go as far as to invalidate our own understanding of the truth – at the least it dulls our innate wisdom. That said, I realize that seeking the company and guidance of those who are wiser than us is important. Good friends and good company are a great form of protection, keeping us safe from the trap of dependency.

An image that comes to mind is the image of the swan. In India, a swan is considered to be quite a mystical creature. A swan is said to be able to differentiate between stones and pearls lying on a river bed, and is able to pick out and keep the pearls. Symbolically, therefore, the swan is used to represent an ability to discern that which is valuable from that which is not. This same power to discern is part of the aspect of the human soul called the intellect.

If human beings also cultivate the power of discernment, we will never be deceived nor will we deceive anyone. With this power we can overcome all falsehood. By cultivating the ability to discern what is needed at any moment in time, we can be both full of love and at the same time lawful. Very often we apply the rule of law when we should be loving, and vice versa. In order to master this ability to discern, we must first become friends with our inner self. When we have a friendship with ourselves, then everyone else can also easily become a friend – and in the end we have no enemies. When all beings are our friends, feelings of equality emerge and dependency is removed.

In the previous chapter we looked at the word "power" – and how it is often misunderstood. Spiritual power, we said, means staying free from influence, and equips us to stand on our own feet, able to make our own wise choices. Another aspect of spiritual power is staying free from dependencies – not just on human beings, but also on habits, addictions and other forms of behaviour that might have held us in bondage for a long time. Think about all the different things that your soul might have become dependent on – certainly people, but also possessions, substances, or more subtle things like emotions such as anger and greed. These last two are very much part of the story of dependency.

MY OWN STORY

As I developed my own relationship with the Supreme and I drew that power within myself, I became better able to value myself. I was able to return to a state of self-esteem and, with this, my own inner dignity emerged and I found I had the power to allow myself to become free – free from any dependency on humans, free from dependency on substances, and free from many subtle addictions, too. Anger no longer holds me in its grip but, rather, thanks to spiritual power, I am now its master. Very often there is a moment in which one can have a choice and can see how two very different attitudes could arise within the self. In a particular situation I saw that I could either react and lift my hand in anger and say harsh things that would inevitably lead toward pain and sorrow, or I could remain very calm, very peaceful and simply let go. And at that moment of choice, because I had spiritual power, it is obvious which direction I chose to move in! And yet, of course, if I had lacked in spiritual power, I wouldn't even have recognized that I had a choice at that point; I would simply have given way to the current emotion, and the reaction that wells up after I had lifted my hand or said things that are not pleasant. Of course, I would feel the impact of this myself later and experience sorrow and regret.

I have described one situation here, but similar patterns occur again and again in our lives and so having spiritual power means being the master of the self, having a choice and being able to move in the right direction. Now, when I practise this in my life, I am able to look at myself with respect.

DEVELOPING YOUR OWN DISCERNING VIEWPOINT

So in order to be wiser and in touch with your innate spiritual power, it is vital, especially at the present moment, to be able to discern. This will help you to steer a course through those daily moments of confusion, when you ask yourself, "What is right, what is wrong; what is true, what is false?" As the global village has become a reality and there has been a cross-fertilization of cultures it has been beautiful to see new communication and interaction through all the different barriers that traditionally existed. But the down side has been that sometimes we have lost our anchor and no longer have basic criteria with which to tell right from wrong. By developing your own inner link with the Supreme you will find that your conscience becomes clear, powerful and centred and that you are able to have a real understanding of the different factors that inform every decision you need to make and every new opportunity of interaction that presents itself. You then are able to evaluate and discern clearly.

Following on, from that, you are able to decide what you need to do. Both the power to discern and the power to decide – to judge what your next step has to be – are vital steps at the present time. Because when, today, you make a decision for yourself, it's not only for yourself. This is a decision that's going to impact on many others around you. The course of action you decide on is not just a decision for today, either; it might well be a decision that will have repercussions 20 years down the line. When you sow a seed, the fruits don't appear at once or even just once; those seeds might bring fruits for many, many years to come; indeed, for many generations to come. And so you need clarity to be able to understand and discern and, furthermore, you need the power to be able to make your decision and then take the necessary steps to implement it. In a world that's moving very rapidly and in which change is accelerating all the time, let these two qualities – clarity and spiritual power – become the guiding force in your life.

As you develop these aspects in your life, you will find that another power has grown up alongside them – the power or wisdom to be able to face all circumstances. You are not able to change the circumstances around you but, yet, if you have spiritual power then you are well equipped to face all the circumstances that appear in front of you.

Look around the world today and you'll see that one of the major causes of distress, pain, war and conflict revolves around discrimination. Developing your powers of discernment will also help you to conquer this and so affect the lives of those you come into contact with in a positive way. One of the major factors causing discrimination is lack of self-respect. Where there is self-respect there is no discriminatory behaviour, and where there is no self-respect then of course we exert the pressure of discrimination on others because of our own inferiority complexes. Not only in social situations, but during our day-to-day dealings with other individuals, the same factors are at work.

Being wise means learning to live with respect and treating others with respect, not with demands, authority, possessiveness or other results of attachment. When we are free from attachment and are in touch with our spiritual power we influence every situation and social interaction with love, purity and joy. We create an atmosphere in which souls can come together in harmony. The power and energy that emerges from us makes life comfortable for others, in a natural and easy way. We might compare it to the power or energy we plug into to access electricity for light, to warm or cool ourselves and generally make life more civilized. In the same way, spiritual power means having the sort of energy that makes life comfortable, humane or even – taking a step further still – divine.

The potential of the human soul is for divinity. It is possible for us to return to that powerful state if we will only free ourselves from our attachments and dependencies.

MEDITATION

Reaching to the Source of power within myself, and in this awareness of my original spiritual identity, I connect with the Almighty Authority. And from God, light and might flow into the self.

I fill myself with the light of love and the power of purity. And as God's power flows within the soul, my mind becomes still... the soul is cleansed... and the power of purity radiates.

God's light and might radiates into the universe. In this way, every time I connect with the Source, I fill myself with power... and that power of love... that power of peace is shared with the world.

PART 10

LISTENING TO YOUR CONSCIENCE

*"If your actions have been according to your conscience,
they will be your protection."*

Often our conscience tells us something and yet we don't listen to
or follow its guidance, and the reality of our life becomes something
else altogether. When our conscience and life are not aligned, it is
not possible to have a mind that is peaceful. When we *do* listen to
that soft, gentle voice of our conscience – which is the seat of our
inner wisdom – and we have the courage to follow its guidance,
then we bring about the inner alignment that allows the mind to
stay very calm.

Conscience relates to everything we are involved in, from our
work and outside activities to our relationships. A sage once said
that one cannot be in a state of peace just by cutting oneself off
from the world, but that by being in the world and doing things the
way they should be done, one can experience peace. We need to
live alongside others to be able to see what is going on within our
conscience.

One of the very powerful aspects that attracted me to Raja Yoga
in the early days was the question of what it is that influences
our conscience. I had observed that what one is told is right and
wrong in one part of the world can be different – and sometimes

quite different – from what is considered right and wrong in other parts of the world. One culture says this is right and another culture says this is wrong. So are we just drifting and shifting every moment day by day, or is there an anchor to ground us and provide a constant reference point for our conscience and which we can build our life upon?

Human conscience is part of the soul. If this is true, then it is not just eternal but is also universal; common to all of us wherever we live and to whichever faith group we belong. If we were to look upon human beings as souls rather than bodies, we would see the beauty, dignity, goodness and the wisdom of everyone because these are the qualities of every soul. Every one of us – not just sages and saints – has goodness, truth, purity, peace and love within ourselves.

Since we are all the same in essence, so human conscience works the same in everyone. Sometimes, if there is a disaster, there is a great upsurge of compassion in everyone's heart. Then the outpouring of support, generosity and help can be huge. This is an indication that when human hearts – and consciences – are touched, then geography, culture, religion, gender and race do not matter. The support of the human family pours forth instantly. That is proof to me that the natural state of every human conscience is one of goodness. We should not have to wait for tragedy to strike to see the goodness of the human spirit!

However, values generally do seem to have become eroded gradually over time. If a carpet is not cleaned every day, it collects dust and within a few days we might declare that the room is not comfortable any more. The accumulation of dust is just a natural form of entropy. In the same way, the human conscience collects negativity simply by being exposed to the sorrow reported in newspapers or by listening to gossip and other less admirable forms of human expression. Perhaps we need to check where our personal values are. Have they ascended or have they descended? If we see the overall trend as downward, then perhaps the state of conscience guiding us isn't as strong or as powerful as it used to be. It is as if we stopped listening to this wise friend inside us, and so, over time, it gave up speaking to us. Every time we ignored the voice of our conscience, that voice became softer and quieter to the point that it didn't speak any more. Even though deep within the heart we know what the truth is, if we don't follow our conscience, it is not possible for the mind to be quiet. When we do start listening to the voice of our conscience again, our mind will become more peaceful and we will feel light and free.

To understand a little more about how this works, think about a situation which sends your mind into upheaval; visualize the state of confusion this creates and the all the pressure and tension you feel. We all know about the impact of stress, tension and burnout on body and mind. Now, in contrast, visualize your mind when it is free from tension. How much more clear, calm and quiet does it feel? Consider the impact of those two states of mind – confused and tense or full of quiet clarity – on your feelings, your life and your relationships. This is the power of the clear conscience – it ensures that the mind moves easily and is able to stay on an even keel.

If we go deep inside our being during meditation, we can get in touch with the truth of our conscience. In this awareness of truth, the conscience is powerful and free from outside influence. Here, we can hear its voice loudly, and if we value what it has to tell us, we feel empowered and have the courage and faith in the truth of its pronouncements. If we choose always to follow the course of action suggested by the conscience – this is the choice of wisdom – we need never experience any sorrow in our heart and neither will we ever feel deceived by anyone. But if we choose not to listen to or follow the conscience, we will have sorrow in the heart, and then the mind will not be peaceful, the intellect will lose its ability to listen to the conscience, and memories of the past will trouble us. When the intellect listens to our conscience, it will be stable and powerful. The wise have a stable intellect – and with this comes the power to be honest.

MY OWN STORY

Where does the conscience come from and how does it develop? It may be part of the mind, but what is its source? In answering this, I find it useful to go back to basics and ask, "What actually produces my thoughts?"

If we have four people all within the same situation, the stimulus on them may be the same, but the responses of each individual to that situation will be very different. For example if there is a major accident, suddenly, almost as if from nowhere, a number of different people descend on the scene. One of them moves toward the victims, checking their pulse and feeling their heart – from his movements and actions you can deduce that he has a medical background. Another person appears on the scene, and his interest is looking at the vehicles. Are they moving, are they able to move, what needs to happen? He's examining the debris and working out the best way to clear the scene. Another person arrives, and his concern is with the situation, but from a different angle. He asks many questions, "Were you here? Did you see? What time did it happen? Was he driving at a fast speed?" And you can understand that this person has some sort of policing background. Yet another person arrives, and she simply cries. She is not able to do anything else, she just cries, and again you assume that she has a personal involvement, that she has a relationship with victim. So, four different people, same situation – different responses.

Their different responses to the external stimulus must be the result of some information recorded within their own inner being, which caused them to behave in a particular way. In any given situation the stimulus comes from outside, but it pushes the buttons within me; on the basis of that I respond with thoughts, and then words and actions. What I am beginning to see is that within myself, I carry very specific information. This information is actually the sum total of all my experiences in the past. In Hindi this is described as *sanskaras* or it could be described as personality traits. Out of the foundation of my *sanskaras*, my own imprints, I create thought.

Once thoughts have been created there are two different possibilities. Firstly, I look at the thought and I agree that yes, this thought should be made manifest; I should allow this thought to be expressed in words or deeds. However, it may also happen that certain thoughts arise and I'm detached enough to be able to observe them, and I decide that these thoughts are not appropriate to be put into action. So another part of my inner self has the capacity to distance the self from the mind and personality, review the situation and come to a judgement. This aspect of the inner being is called the *buddhi* – the intellect or conscience. When the conscience comes into play and is alive, it has the power to lead the mind in the right direction. It has the power to actually select which aspects of personality must be manifest, and which other aspects have to sit quietly for now, and may be expressed later.

These three faculties of the self can be seen in terms of layers. So, the superficial layer is made up of the mind and thoughts. It takes only a moment to look inside and access the quality of my thinking – negative, positive or something in-between. The next layer is the *buddhi*, the intellect or conscience. The deepest layer is this bedrock of experience. We describe this as the personality of the self. When we speak of personality, it is useful to think of it as an iceberg – you can see only one tenth; nine tenths are hidden below the surface.

It takes me time to even know myself, and it definitely requires a lot of time to try and know others. But the more I know myself, the easier it becomes to change myself and listen to my conscience.

GROWING YOUR OWN CONSCIENCE

It is useful to think about these aspects of the self as layers, which we can gradually work on one by one. But it's also helpful to understand them as part of a cycle. You have a thought, put that thought into action, the action creates an imprint and the imprint creates a further thought. I have left one very valuable aspect out of this equation, because in life today we generally do leave it out. Today, thought leads to action, action leads to reaction, reaction leads to thought. We get caught up in this cycle of cause and effect. But it becomes a trap, because a significant factor has been omitted. Between thought and action comes one little extra step – a moment to pause and reflect. We want everything so instantly today that mostly we forget to reflect. But in order to start listening to your conscience, once a thought comes you must ask the question, "Is this right or not?" In that one moment of pausing and stopping to engage the intellect, you start to break the cycle and get in touch with your wise intellect.

So firstly your intellect has to become powerful enough to be able to perceive the reality of the situation, and to step in and say, "I can see what's really going on... stop!" In addition, your intellect needs to have the power to implement this decision. Sometimes we can understand that the mind isn't moving us in the right direction, and yet we still allow ourselves to be pulled into negative situations. So how do you gain the power to act on what your conscience points out?

Today we seem to have handed over this power completely. We rarely make decisions for ourselves and no longer follow through our decisions. We have stopped listening to the soft, still voice of our conscience. If you ignore the sound of your conscience once, twice or three times, you can see what is going to happen. The conscience will go to sleep and not offer any opinion. So from a state of morality you come close to a state not only of immorality, but of "amorality" – the present condition of the world – in which it is considered OK to say, "It doesn't really matter; there isn't really such a thing as black and white, everything is just a blurred grey."

Yet if you cultivate spirituality and knowledge of your self you awaken your intellect. And this is the way to free yourself from addiction. Not just the obvious substance addictions, but also the subtle inner spiritual addictions we all suffer from. When you begin to meditate you are able to absorb a great deal of power through the meditation, which can express itself as willpower. Your appraisal of your life changes, your motivation changes, and you begin to take steps in the correct direction. For example, every time you give way to the habit of ego, or to anger or to attachment, that addiction develops and grows, and ultimately has a strangling effect. If you can exercise choice and allow the conscience to intervene – and through meditation make the conscience so powerful that its understanding is actually practised – you break the vicious trap and are able to be free. The thought comes and, if necessary, you dismiss that thought. You don't allow it to be filtered into action. If a good thought comes and you decide that it is right, you allow it to be expressed though activity. So as an ongoing process, the goodness is reinforced and the negative is gradually erased. All of this simply requires understanding, awareness and practice. You can practise the awareness of the soul in meditation, but it's vitally important to continue the experiment by listening to your conscience as you walk, move about your day and do all the activities that are necessary in your life.

MEDITATION

Sitting quietly, I move my thoughts away from my own body, human beings and possessions, and I come back to my spiritual identity... the identity of the self... and I find that point of peace within.

And as I look at myself in the state of peace, I understand that my conscience has to be activated. Knowing myself as a spiritual being gives new life to my conscience, so that it awakens. In this state of awareness – with my conscience awake and clear – strength grows and I am able to discern truth. And in the state of peace and stability, not only do I understand truth, but I have the capacity to be able to follow the path of truth: truth within my thoughts... truth within my words... truth within my actions... always truth.

As a silent, detached observer of myself, I see the darkness of ignorance leave... I watch the light of truth grow... and, as truth returns to my own inner being, I am able to have regard for myself. Having this power of truth and respect, I am free at last. No more dependencies... no more desires... no more attachments. Truth is within my own inner being... purity is my original state of being... in my original state I am pure, I am clean.

Seeing myself in this condition, I appreciate myself... I love myself and joy springs within my heart. I return to my own original state of goodness. I know I am a unique and valuable being. Keeping this awareness, I come back to the awareness of my role in life, but I bring back this inner dignity and self-esteem to guide me in the roles that I play.

PART 11

DEVELOPING HONESTY AND TRUTH

*"To tolerate and maintain good wishes in the face
of adversity requires tremendous inner strength.
However, the rewards are great."*

All real success in life is due to honesty. When we trust ourselves, others have trust in us and God is also with us. Someone once said to me, "I don't trust anyone, so what can I do?" I replied, "Become trustworthy. Become worthy of the trust of others." The proof of our honesty is that we are trustworthy in our dealings. Another person should never come us and our sense of honesty.

But in order to remain honest, we need great wisdom. We may think we are honest, but that is not the same thing as saying the first thing that enters the mind! Only after delving more deeply into the subject will we be able to do everything with absolutely accuracy in accordance with our honesty. Our own honesty will only be visible to ourselves when we have no selfish motives left in our relationships and we can be co-operative with everyone. When we are honest, we no longer deceive anyone or take sides. Only when we have a friendship with every one we encounter will there be friendliness in our relationships and honesty in our actions. Then our actions will be decent and filled with virtue. That is the sign of wisdom.

When we remain honest, three other virtues come about: patience, tolerance and contentment. The three qualities are interlinked. Those who become impatient, for example, lack in tolerance and can never be content. And if someone doesn't do something well and we become upset (and lose our inner contentment and patience), it reveals a lack of tolerance. To truly be tolerant means never saying that we are tolerating something, but internally maintaining the ability to be content. In impatience there is so much loss. And so it is always better to say nothing than to speak out about anything that is done even slightly wrong. The one who has patience is able to remain cheerful, mature, humble, peaceful and calm; and the one who is content will feel happy and think whatever he has is his good fortune.

These values are very useful for those who wish to remain honest in life – indeed, it is only by cultivating these that the soul becomes really virtuous. Those who are wise take these three pills every morning: patience, tolerance and contentment. They then become the few who have understood wisdom and enable thousands of others to understand, too, through their example.

In honesty there is real happiness as well as wisdom. If we accumulate money in an honest way, for example, we may continue to eat and live very simply but we will be happy because we have not committed any wrongdoing. We can remain simple and honest; we don't need to live like a king or queen in order to feel happy. Happiness is not dependent on external things. If we think and behave in such an honest way that others become happy with us, then we will definitely continue to be happy within ourselves.

Those who do not chose this path of wisdom will have sorrow in their hearts – and their brains will become tired, too. If we are tempted to give up honesty, then we will keep thinking that something is not good, or that something is not right. But if we learn to keep the heart happy, then the brain will remain fresh and we will not feel tired. We will have the inspiration and energy to perform good actions and create continuous happiness for ourselves.

If we feel pressure in a relationship, it means there is an absence of honesty as well as of love in that relationship. When there is truth, love is automatically there. Love always lives in a clean heart. Truth makes us the natural embodiment of love and we become fearless and free from animosity. Whenever fear is experienced, the power of truth is absent.

So by accurately using truth and understanding, we stay happy. Truth and honesty bring so much personal power that we are able to tolerate anything that confronts us so that we can completely accept the things that have already happened, and adjust ourselves to meet the future with honest contentment. Honesty is the foundation of wisdom in relationships and interactions, and truth is the foundation of wisdom within ourselves.

MY OWN STORY

How do I develop my honesty on a day-to-day level? I first of all accept responsibility for everything I have done. Secondly, I stop any guilt trip! I do not allow myself to wallow in self-pity by experiencing guilt and sorrow. Instead, through meditation, I come to a point of realization, and I gather power and love from God so that I can transform and reform myself. I maintain my sense of dignity, too, knowing that I am God's child, and grasp the opportunity for honest transformation and change. This process of becoming more truthful involves forgiving the self and allowing the self to forget. Having learnt the lessons of the past, it is important to be able to let go and forget. If I haven't forgiven myself, of course, it will be impossible to forget.

I apply this formula first to myself. I have to learn to forgive myself; I have to learn to forget my past misdeeds and be free of the bondage of the past. Then I can do that which is good and true – with God's love and God's help. Then I have to apply that same formula to my relationships with others. Let me have a heart that is big enough to be able to forgive. Carrying resentment in the heart pollutes my awareness and my feelings – it stops me from behaving with honesty – so I allow God's love instead to make me so open and generous that I can forgive. It also helps to know that just as I am changing, others are changing too, so I choose not to see them through a vision of their past. If I am able to forget the past and give other people the space to show me their new personality and new outlook, then I can create a new relationship with them. If I give them space, this becomes possible. If I hang onto the past, it becomes a block.

GROWING YOUR OWN HONESTY

It is human nature to ignore the truth. It is easier to point the finger outward and say that someone else is to blame for the ills we encounter in life. And yet every time you point one finger, three fingers point back at you: your thoughts (you are responsible for these); your feelings (your thoughts are responsible for your emotions); and the choices you make (you are responsible for your decisions and so for the results of those decisions). It is much easier to shed responsibility and say the government, or the United Nations, or society, or your parents or even God are responsible. And yet the reality is that it is very much you who are responsible.

However, understanding and accepting this honest responsibility is not a burdensome thing. Rather, understanding and accepting this responsibility is the gift of empowerment. Because it is through this understanding that you then have the power to change the situation you find yourself in. Once you know that you are responsible for your thoughts and feelings and choices, you can consciously change the pattern of your thinking to bring about truthful feelings and choices instead of negative ones. You don't need to wait for somebody else to try and cheer you up; you don't have to wait for somebody to bring you chocolates and flowers. This might never happen! And even if it did happen one day, it is not going to continue happening every day. So what you *can* do is to very simply change the quality and pattern of your thinking and create good thoughts. By sowing the seeds of good thoughts, you will create a harvest and receive the fruit of good feelings.

In the same way, in a situation which you find difficult, ask the following question, "Well, what am I supposed to learn here? What is this scene within the cosmic drama teaching me?" Once you understand the lesson you can change your attitude, then change your course of action – and in doing so you will find that you have changed your circumstances and also changed your world around you so that everything is more honest and full of truth. This is the law of karma, which we will investigate further in chapter 12. When we follow our conscience with honesty and accept responsibility we have the key to create situations of our choice – to create the destiny of our choice. We come to the understanding that no unseen forces are controlling and manipulating us; that would lead to a state of constant fear and bondage. Understanding karma means opening up the door to the treasure of our own destiny and choosing what we would like to have. The way in which we think determines the way in which we behave and act, and so karma starts inside – with our honest truthfulness – and then we see the effects it generates outside. We again feel the impact and repercussions of that situation inside, so we think, consult our conscience, and act again. Understanding this inner and outward and outward and inner journey is the way to achieve constant happiness in life. This is wisdom.

MEDITATION

Sitting quietly I turn within. I am a point of light... I am a soul. In this awareness of I, the soul, I emerge, from within my own being, the quality of peace. Peace exists within myself... peace is mine... and in this state of peace, with my mind very calm and collected, I ask myself some questions. What is there within me?

Looking deep I am able to go below the surface of all the accumulation of rubbish and I discover the beauty within. In my original state there is beauty within the soul. I am eternal... I am light... I am peace... I am divine.

In this awareness, looking out into the world, I see every other human being as a divine being, a being of light... and I send vibrations of peace to each one of my brothers. I come back... back into the awareness of my physical costume, my physical surroundings, but I keep this consciousness of eternity... of light and peace.

PART 12

CHOOSING HAPPINESS

"Success comes when you are content with yourself,
when your activities bring contentment, and when
everyone else is content with you."

Happiness is not something we should experience just occasionally. We can choose to be happy all the time. Even in the midst of adverse situations, why should we lose our happiness?

Sometimes we can be overcome by feelings of unhappiness even though there is no apparent cause. At other times a very small situation occurs but the sadness we feel can be disproportionately overwhelming. We should understand that each one of us internally has a store of sorrow that has accumulated over a long period of time and it sometimes comes to the surface. At times like that, we tend to feel quite disconnected from others. This is why it is important to do the work of clearing out these feelings of sorrow. This allows our wisdom to continue growing and to come to fruition.

When we are in a state of sadness all our enthusiasm just disappears. There is a sense of being worthless, of no use. We become disheartened. We begin to compare ourselves with others and feel that we are just not capable of doing the things they can do. At that time it is as if sadness is ruling us. What is more, people tend to keep away from those who are sad and miserable. Sadness therefore is detrimental to our inner wisdom. It can even become a habit. So we need to make effort not to allow ourselves to become sad; we need immediately to change the way we are thinking. We have to say to ourselves, "I can do it. God will help me." We have to chase the sadness away. If a testing situation occurs, we should cultivate the attitude that this is only a temporary state.

But while such situations may come and go, what will stay are the impressions that our reactions to them have left on other people. This is another reason for not allowing such situations to get us down. If our interactions with others and our own behaviour during times of sadness have been good, then others will have taken benefit and comfort from that situation.

The subtle reason behind our loss of happiness is that we have been tempted to follow a wrong trend of thought. Sometimes, by dwelling on a situation too much we make it bigger than it actually is. So, if we can use our thoughts to make that which is small, big, then surely we should be able to use our thoughts to do the opposite, too? With the right thoughts, it is possible to make something big, small. In other words, to change a mountain into a mustard seed!

It is important that we don't simply become satisfied with the happiness that comes from external achievements. It shouldn't be that if someone praises us we feel happy but then if they don't praise us, we don't feel happy. We need to have an unshakeable positive belief in ourselves. We need an attitude in which we feel "Of course, I can do this!" and do not have the slightest doubt about whether we can achieve something or not, even if others fail to wish us well.

This does not mean we need to become obsessive perfectionists – this is not a wise state to live in – but simply that we use our inner wisdom to know we are doing our best. Then we won't need to look to others for praise because, having done our best, inside we will experience contentment.

When we make effort to detach ourselves from situations, by going beyond them, then it becomes possible to maintain happiness. It is as if the situation gets left down below and cannot reach or touch us. However badly something is going down below, from up above it seems small and insignificant. Just look from above and everything will seem possible. This is what is meant by the term, "rise above it". This then allows us to gather speed in our effort.

To maintain happiness, we need to study, practise and experience. Our practice needs to be instant. When we hear something that will be useful to the soul, we should begin to practise it immediately. That practice will strengthen our intellect and bring experience and inner power. We will then have the feeling that something we had lost is being restored. Our heart will feel such gratitude and we will feel so fortunate that the happiness we thought we had lost has returned. Now it cannot disappear because we have changed.

Maintaining such an attitude might seem a tall order, but it is not such a big thing to change. Once our attention is drawn to something, we can be wise enough to change. But when it comes to changing something about ourselves, we need to be sure that we are not doing so just to please someone else. When we change, let it be because we recognize the importance of good quality actions.

Then we will experience so much happiness that past sorrows end and no matter what happens in the present we remain happy and can deal with situations that might arise in the future. True happiness can only be experienced in the present and if it comes from past situations or from expectation of future events, it is dependent on something outside our inner self.

Our happiness shouldn't be ordinary. It should be a happiness that is filled with power. There should be such power in our happiness that we can help others become happy – that is the wisdom and the fruit of our happiness.

MY OWN STORY

As I began to practise meditation, I become aware that meditation and life go together hand in hand, leading to happiness. One cannot be divorced from the other. Meditation influences my lifestyle; my lifestyle affects my meditation. And so I became aware of *karma*, or action. In fact, another term for Raja Yoga is "karma yoga" – or having a link with God that influences the quality of my actions. The soul and body function together in the world and the purpose of the soul taking on a physical body is to express itself in action – through thoughts, words and deeds. Having done this, I then receive the return of those thoughts, words and deeds. This is described as the law of action and reaction. Whatever I put out comes back to me as a reaction. Whatever cause I initiate, I experience the effect. This law of causality – the law of action leading to reaction – is described as the law of karma. The Sanskrit word *karma* simply means action without any connotation of the quality of the action involved. And so karma yoga indicates that when there a true state of yoga, or link with God, then the experiences I have in my meditation are expressed in the quality of my actions, and the quality of my actions determine to what extent I experience a relationship with God.

This particular form of yoga is such a simple form of inner connection of the soul with God through my thoughts and feelings that I am able to maintain consciousness of my connection with God as I go about my daily duties. So yoga can take place while I am engaged in karma. It is obviously important to spend a few minutes in silence daily, but it is important also to continue that awareness through my daily life.

Even as a little child, maybe at the age of two, I learned about karma – we all do – though of course I didn't refer to it using that term. I threw a ball and watched it come bouncing back. In certain scriptures this has been described as sowing and reaping. As you sow, so shall you reap. It is one of the absolute laws of the universe – and in fact it is because of this law that the universe keeps ticking on. It is not possible to say which was the very first action that took place, just as it is not possible to say whether it was the acorn that came first or the oak that came first. Which is it? Is it the seed then the tree? Or is it the tree and then the seed? If we ponder such thoughts, we begin to see a cycle, an eternal pattern, continuing and ongoing.

If I wish to have a life in which there is constant happiness, then I need to know which seeds I must sow in order to receive the fruit of happiness. Action begins with the quality of my thoughts. For example, if I pick a bunch of flowers and I present them to you, on one level that action seems a very sweet, very loving action. And yet, of course, my body language, the expression in my eyes, my attitude and the thrust of my hands all give you an indication as to the extent of my love or the integrity of my love or whether the flowers are being offered for another reason than love entirely. Maybe a bunch of flowers is a symbolic act asking for forgiveness. Maybe the bunch of flowers is saying, "I want your attention." Maybe this little bunch of flowers is speaking very loudly saying, "If I give you this, what are you going to give back to me?" Maybe it is part of an agreement, a contract that I want you to engage in. The bunch of flowers can say whatever I want it to say. It depends on what is happening in my inner world – karma is totally governed by consciousness and motivation. So, although the action in itself may be a very simple one – offering flowers – the motive behind the action creates the quality within the action and thereby determines the result of the action. You know sometimes we say, "I did so much to try and help so-and-so and they just were not grateful." Well let me step back for a moment. Who was trying to do what? Who was actually giving what? What was the motive behind all that? If the motive was genuinely one of sympathy, empathy and concern there should not be any question of being grateful. I have given out of the openness and the goodness of my heart without setting a price on the act. I am not expecting a return for it. And yet, of course, one can see that in today's world this very rarely happens. A constant charge is placed on whatever we do. We have put a price tag on even the most simple of acts and expect something in return.

GROWING YOUR OWN HAPPINESS

The reality of today's world is that karma has become corrupt. Our motives have become mixed and so we experience a great deal of pain and suffering. In a very simple way, one can differentiate karma on different levels. There is good karma – *sukarma* – the karma by which you can give happiness. Secondly there is *akarma* – neutral karma – an action without negative or positive feedback. The third type of karma is *vikarma* – action based on negativity, or vices. The result of the latter is, of course, pain and suffering. If you look over 24 hours and try to assess which category of karma your actions fall into, you'll probably find that the balance is a little top heavy. The *vikarma*, the negative karma, may have taken over to the extent that there are very few flashes of *sukarma*, of that karma with which happiness can be generated.

Through the practice of meditation – coming back to the awareness of I, the soul – and maintaining your link with God, *sukarma*, good karma, becomes a way of life. One reason for this is that the whole equation of giving and taking changes. In my experience of the link with God, I access an ocean of love and happiness, peace and power, and I can absorb from it as much and as many of these positive qualities as I choose. There are no limits placed on this whatsoever. It means I no longer ask for anything from human beings. If you do the same, you will no longer need to wait for human beings to give you anything; you will no longer be dependent on human beings. Instead, as you have taken from the source so you will be able to give – offering love and happiness, and sharing peace – and so your actions are consistently *sukarma*. To whatever extent you maintain the eternal awareness of the soul and your link with God, you will be able to maintain the quality of your karma in this category of good karma. But the moment you fall into amnesia and forget who you are, returning into the limited consciousness of the body, your link with God is broken and the channel of love is severed. So, your actions inevitably fall into *vikarma*, bad karma, because they are motivated by a very limited consciousness. When you think of "I" and "mine" in limited terms you automatically become influenced by things like ego, greed, desires and attachments. And so your actions become *vikarma*. This adds to the burdens you carry, causes sorrow to others and only increases the burden of sorrow for yourself. There is very little opportunity at the present moment of doing *akarma* – neutral karma. Even in actions on one level that could be neutral, for instance caring for the body – looking after it with food, drink and sleep – are tainted with *vikarma* if you see yourself on a physical level only, without awareness of eternity. Everything depends on awareness or amnesia. In amnesia we forget and there is *vikarma*. In awareness we remember and there is the possibility of good karma.

And so the subject of karma need not be complex or complicated – it can be extremely simple. We can check ourselves. Am I soul-conscious? Am I aware of being a child of God? If I am, my karma will automatically be very good. This is the route to happiness. The property that God the Father gives me is that of joy and happiness. In this relationship of Father and child I claim happiness as my birthright. This is my treasure store. I can multiply it, I can share it, I can donate it, but it remains mine for ever and ever, and while I keep this treasure with me, no pain or sorrow can ever touch me. Let us spend a few minutes looking inward and thinking about the freedom that comes with happiness.

MEDITATION

Let us now turn inward, and awaken the original quality of happiness, of joy within the self.

Sitting quietly, with one thought I focus my attention on the soul: I, the eternal being... the being of peace. In this awareness of peace, I move beyond the limits of my physical body; and in this state of peace, I begin my journey. I dive below the surface of the waves to discover the treasures within. On the surface are the memories of the immediate experiences of the past, but patiently I decide for a while not to ponder these; not to spend my valuable moments of silence contemplating memories of sorrow. I decide to see what there is further down... deeper within.

The waves remain up above, and the silence of my own inner being draws me towards itself, and as I come to the core of my being, I see that here, at the very heart of my being, there is beauty... there is love... and I can feel happiness emerging from deep inside. I begin to touch the treasure of joy, knowing that this is my eternal state. I maintain this inner awareness of happiness.

PART 13

ENJOYING THE FRUITS OF WISDOM

"Wisdom brings everything –
heart, wealth, happiness and harmony."

Wisdom lends us a tremendous strength and stability – and this allows a wise person to be an anchor, not only for one's own life, but also for the lives of many others around us. Wisdom is like the trunk of a great tree – its strength is always available to give support to others. But wisdom does not have to make our lives too serious. Wisdom, in fact, can bring a great deal of laughter and love into our lives. I have observed many times how wise people are able to tiptoe through the dangerous minefields of many situations in today's world and laugh about things that other people would find problematic. Instead of being dismayed by problems, wise people simply smile and say, "Yes that is a challenge, but it is a challenge that can help me to move on in life." Wisdom has filled the lives of those who choose to nurture it with a great deal of lightness and love and joy – and if lightness and love and joy are the things we are looking for in life, then wisdom is definitely the key!

At the point at which wisdom becomes important to us and we decide that this is what we want in our lives, then many changes begin to take place quite naturally – in a very beautiful but also a dramatic way. Wisdom is definitely divine and it carries us to our own state of divinity.

But in order to arrive at this point we need to be truly aware of ourselves – to understand the eternal identity of the soul. Secondly, we need to sit in silence and experiment with the awareness of being a soul. The more we experiment with this, the more we come to appreciate the truth that in reality each of us is a being of light. Through this practice and this experience we become the master – master of our own feelings and able to be selective about which parts of our personality or emotions we would like to express in any given situation. We also come to master our own thoughts, being able to choose the direction we want them to go in, and able to turn the mind inward when necessary. As we begin to do this, we discover the treasures of inner wisdom. So often in life we spend a lifetime searching for the experience of a moment of peace, a moment of love, a glimpse of happiness, or a moment of real knowing. And yet sometimes even a momentary experience of this eludes us. But with the key of soul-consciousness and this method of turning inward, these treasures are available to us at any moment.

MY OWN STORY

When I began to enjoy knowing myself in this way, I realized that I had forgotten the sweetness of my own nature; I had grown accustomed to feeling and seeing all the rough and raw edges of my personality and so I had forgotten to appreciate myself. I had definitely lost all love for myself. In fact, I had become a stranger to myself. But now I know I am peace and I am light, I have become a friend for myself. Looking at myself peacefully, I began to appreciate the beauty of my inner being. In my original state, I am filled with truth, with wisdom and with beauty. I can see goodness within myself; and now my appreciation of my own value has grown. I know that I as an individual am unique. So I began to love myself; and, in this awareness of my eternal identity, and loving myself, I am now able to let go of the bondage and chains of guilt from the past.

Now I can be free: I am able at last to learn from the past and yet forget. I can forgive myself; and so the burden of sorrow and guilt is removed, and I enjoy the beauty of loving myself. I look outward equipped with this new, wise attitude toward myself, and I find that my vision of the world has changed. My perspective on other individuals, other souls, is very different now. I see each being not simply in terms of their human frame, but also as a being of light, like myself, a wise being with whom I am connected eternally. I can see the recent interaction and the exchanges of yesterday and the day before, but I choose not to hold on to the immediate past or even the long-distant past. I choose to see a being of light, and my eternal connection with this being. We are all sisters and brothers, and our link together is the link of love.

Aware of love for my eternal self, all my other feelings have been transformed and I can send out thoughts and feelings and vibrations of love. This love reaches the people I have an intimate connection with. This love also reaches every human being in the world. I can send out thoughts of love out into every corner of the universe. Thoughts of love touch the elements of the environment, and the power of this love is such that it can even cleanse and heal nature itself. All this comes about simply by maintaining my awareness of the eternal being radiating love.

ENJOYING THE FRUIT OF WISDOM
FOR YOURSELF

Thinking about the fruit of wisdom helps us to understand the role of God as Teacher, sharing with us the secrets of eternity, of creation, of the universe and of ourselves. The Teacher blesses us with wisdom, and in this relationship of love, faith and obedience we can claim wisdom as the blessing from the Supreme Teacher.

The only thing you have to do now is to keep your mind open and clean. If you allow the mind to be polluted with criticism, or by seeing defects or with antagonism, attachments or desires, then you will not be able to absorb the gift of wisdom that the Teacher gives. Your only task is to keep the mind clean and then the great Teacher will fill it with wisdom. It is also important to keep your mind open. One of the deepest traits of human personality is the ego – this one difficulty will be a constant battle in the absorption of wisdom. But if you let go of the ego, cultivate humility and pay attention to the voice of your conscience, you are sure to keep yourself open to learning. As you absorb the wisdom that God blesses us with, that wisdom will become the guiding light for your life.

God's role is threefold: to share knowledge, to offer love and to give us power. And as we human souls recognize God and build a connection and relationship with the divine, so we are able to draw these qualities into our own lives. This process transforms the human spirit and leads it to transform the world with truth, light and wisdom. Now is the time for transformation; today is the time to start receiving those treasures from God. Experiment now by turning within once more and experiencing your own eternal qualities; the divine wisdom that belongs to you, but which you may have forgotten. Spend a few moments in silent meditation so that you come to experience that inner wisdom once again and embrace the power of pure love – love that is the original wise state of being of the eternal self.

MEDITATION

Sitting quietly, I know that I am a soul. I am not my physical body... within a moment, I can turn inward and be a point of light.

In this awareness of my own spiritual identity, I transcend the limits of my physical body; my image of myself has changed. Now, the compartments in which I had placed myself have dissolved: colour, gender, age, race, religion had all become limiting factors for my consciousness. Now I can see so clearly that all of these are not part of I, the eternal wise being. All these are associated with my body... and I decide to go beyond these limits. My image of myself is transformed instantly. I am light... I am peace.

I turn my attention to my eternal identity. I am a soul, not the body. I leave the body sitting quietly and I move beyond into the dimension of light... into the presence of God. God's light... God's love, peace reach the soul. This is my eternal Mother. From my eternal Mother I experience total love and acceptance. I had forgotten this connection, but my Mother had not. I had gone wandering off far away, but my Mother has found me and reminded me.

I face my benevolent Father, the One who has nothing but goodness in His heart for me. I can feel His good wishes, His love, His hopes and aspirations for me. I know that my Father sees me in my perfect form... and the power of His vision enables me to let go of limited things that were tying me down and to accept perfection in my heart. In the presence of God I know perfection is possible.

My Mother, my Father, my Teacher, the Ocean of Knowledge wants to share all secrets with me and blesses me with perfect wisdom. The Teacher keeps nothing back, but allows me access to all treasures so that I can be free and independent.

God becomes my Friend and entertains me and supports me. God's love lifts me to my perfect state... God's light... God's love reaches out into the universe and creates a world of light and love.

ABOUT BK JAYANTI

More than 40 years ago BK Jayanti dedicated her life to the study, practice and teaching of the ancient system of meditation and spiritual understanding known as Raja Yoga. Since then, she has shared with millions of people worldwide her understanding and experience of the deepest spiritual truths. She is European Director of Brahma Kumaris World Spiritual University (BKWSU).

BK Jayanti is sought after as a speaker across the globe because she has a unique ability to impart the deepest spiritual truths with the utmost clarity. As well as talking about and teaching meditation, the lecture themes closest to her heart include health, education, racial harmony, women's needs, the religions of the world, peace and international relations. These interests stem from her personal experience: as a young woman from a traditional Asian family growing up in London, she had to face not only the cultural divide but also gender issues. Her deep understanding of spirituality enabled her to understand the role of feminine qualities in personal and world transformation and empowered her to use these in a practical way.

BK Jayanti places the erosion of spiritual values at the heart of the underlying cause of the crises that the world is facing today, and so she has worked tirelessly to promote positive, human, spiritual values to all sectors of society. In 1980 she was appointed the University's main representative to the United Nations (UN) in Geneva, Switzerland. This has led her to participate in many UN Conferences and projects, in connection with women, development, the environment and youth as well as in a major international project for the United Nations International Year of Peace. As part of this work, she has undertaken extensive research into the role spiritual values play in changing the world.

ABOUT BRAHMA KUMARIS

The Brahma Kumaris World Spiritual University is an international organization working at all levels of society for positive change. Established in 1937, the University now has more than 8,500 centres in over 100 countries.

Acknowledging the intrinsic worth and goodness of the inner self, the University teaches a practical method of meditation that helps people to cultivate their inner strengths and values.

The University has local centres around the world offering courses and seminars that encourage spirituality in daily life and cover topics such as positive thinking, anger management, stress relief and self esteem, amongst others. This spiritual approach is also brought into healthcare, social work, education, prisons and other community settings.

The University's Academy in Mount Abu, Rajasthan, India, offers individuals from all backgrounds a variety of life-long learning opportunities to help them recognize their inherent qualities and abilities in order to make the most of their lives. The University also supports the Global Hospital and Research Centre in Mount Abu.

BRAHMA KUMARIS CENTRES

WORLD HEADQUARTERS
PO Box No 2, Mount Abu 307501, RAJASTHAN, INDIA
Tel: (+91) 2974 - 238261 to 68 Fax: (+91) 2974 - 238883
E-mail: abu@bkivv.org

INTERNATIONAL CO-ORDINATING OFFICE
& REGIONAL OFFICE FOR EUROPE AND THE MIDDLE EAST
Global Co-operation House, 65-69 Pound Lane, London, NW10 2HH, UK
Tel: (+44) 208 727 3350 Fax: (+44) 208 727 3351
E-mail: london@bkwsu.org

AFRICA
Global Museum for a Better World, Maua Close, off Parklands Road,
Westlands, PO Box 123, Sarit Centre, Nairobi, Kenya
Tel: (+254) 20-374 3572 Fax: (+254) 20-374 3885
E-mail: nairobi@bkwsu.org

AUSTRALIA AND SOUTH EAST ASIA
78 Alt Street, Ashfield, Sydney, NSW 2131, Australia
Tel: (+61) 2 9716 7066 Fax: (+61) 2 9716 7795
E-mail: ashfield@au.bkwsu.org

THE AMERICAS AND THE CARIBBEAN
Global Harmony House, 46 S. Middle Neck Road, Great Neck, NY 11021, USA
Tel: (+1) 516 773 0971 Fax: (+1) 516 773 0976
E-mail: newyork@bkwsu.org

RUSSIA, CIS AND THE BALTIC COUNTRIES
2 Gospitalnaya Ploschad, build. 1, Moscow - 111020, Russia
Tel: (+7) 495 263 02 47 Fax: (+7) 495 261 32 24
E-mail: moscow@bkwsu.org

www.bkpublications.com
E-mail: enquiries@bkpublications.com